The Treasure Store
Charles H. Spurgeon

The Best of Charles H. Spurgeon's Writings

The Treasure Store
Charles H. Spurgeon

The Best of Charles H. Spurgeon's Writings

Edited and compiled by
Robert Backhouse

Marshall Pickering
An Imprint of HarperCollinsPublishers

Marshall Pickering is an Imprint of
HarperCollins*Religious*
Part of HarperCollins*Publishers*
77–85 Fulham Palace Road, London W6 8JB

First published in Great Britain
in 1995 by Marshall Pickering

1   3   5   7   9   10   8   6   4   2

© 1995 in this compilation HarperCollins*Publishers*

A catalogue record for this book is
available from the British Library

0 551 02992 7

Printed and bound in Great Britain by
HarperCollinsManufacturing Glasgow

Contents

Introduction

Dr Jim Packer wrote recently:

> As Billy Graham might be described as a giant-size Southern
> Baptist of today's type, so Charles Haddon Spurgeon
> (1834–1892) can be described as a giant-size English Baptist
> of Victorian type . . . 'The Guv'nor', as his colleagues called
> him, was a fascinating human being. A perky countryman, a
> witty depressive, and a self-educated theologian, he was
> hugely intelligent, massively common-sensical, and totally
> masterful in utterance . . . He was a robust saint of the
> Augustinian and Puritan type, who with unflagging freshness
> projected the many-sided relationship between God the
> Creator and the sinners whom he loves and saves through
> Jesus Christ as the most wonderful and important thing in the
> world.[1]

Despite his ordinary family background – his father was an
Independent minister and a coalyard clerk in Essex – Spurgeon
became personal friends with many of the most notable people in
England. The Archbishop of Canterbury sought Spurgeon's
counsel, and the Prime Minister, Gladstone, met and corre-
sponded with Spurgeon as with a friend. People often referred to

Gladstone and Spurgeon as 'the two prime ministers'. It was no rare event for Spurgeon to find himself having breakfast or dinner at No. 10 Downing Street. Whenever news reached Gladstone that Spurgeon was ill, a special messenger from the First Lord of the Treasury was sent with a message of sympathy to Spurgeon.

Spurgeon was held in high esteem by leading Christians on both sides of the Atlantic. D. L. Moody was invited by Spurgeon to preach at his church, the Metropolitan Tabernacle, and from the following extracts from his letters it is easy to see how much the world's most famous evangelist admired Spurgeon:

17 March, 1874
Dear Spurgeon,
Many thanks for your kind note. I am in hopes that you will be led by the Spirit to preach to young men on Sunday next. Enclosed I send you a circular that a minister here is sending out in the hope that it will stir up some interest in Britain.
In regard to my coming to your Tabernacle, I consider it a great honour to be invited; and, in fact, I should consider it an honour to black your boots; but to preach to your people would be out of the question. If they will not turn to God under your preaching, 'neither will they be persuaded, though one rise from the dead'.
    Yours with much love,
        D. L. Moody

The following year Spurgeon helped Moody in his London mission and this next extract from Moody's letter reveals how much Moody appreciated Spurgeon's assistance.

8 May, 1875
Dear Spurgeon,
Ten thousand thanks for your help last night. You gave us a great lift. I wish you would give us every night you can for the next sixty days. There are so few men who can draw on a

week-night, and I want to keep up the meetings in the East End and West at the same time; it is hard on me to have to speak twice the same evening, and yet I shall have to do it next week, for I cannot get anyone for the West End. Do all you can for the work, and we shall see the blessed results.

    Yours in haste,
       D. L. Moody

Six years later Moody shows that he still holds Spurgeon in high esteem, in the following letter that was written because Spurgeon was absent from the Tabernacle, where Moody had agreed to preach.

11 October, 1881
Dear Mr Spurgeon,
Yours of the 9th is to hand, and in reply let me say that I am thankful for your very kind note. It quite touched my heart. I have for years thought more of you than any other man preaching the gospel on this earth, and, to tell you the truth, I shrink from standing in your place. I do not know of a church in all the land that I shrink from as I do from yours – not that your people are not in sympathy with the Gospel that I try to preach, but you can do it so much better than I can.
I thank you for inviting me, and (D.V.) I will be with your good people on November 20. Will you want Mr Sankey, or will your own precentor have charge? Either will suit me.
Remember me to your good wife, and accept my thanks for your letter of cheer.

    Yours truly,
       D. L. Moody

Moody's singing companion, Ira D. Sankey – the George Beverly Shea of the day – wrote this letter of appreciation to Spurgeon:

8 November, 1886
'Dear Beloved,'
Many thanks for the precious word you gave us yesterday [on the subject of 'our Ascended Lord']. It was indeed most refreshing to my soul.
Is it not a beautiful thought that our Lord's disciples always call him, or spoke to him, as the Son of God, while he was down here on earth, and that he always spoke of himself as the Son of Man; but that, when he went up to heaven, John saw him there, and then spoke of him, or called him, the Son of Man? John, no doubt, wanted to hold on to him, even as a brother.
I will try to see you again at the Tabernacle before I sail on the 18th;
    I love you very much, God bless you and yours!
        Ira D. Sankey

The leading British philanthropist and social reformer, Lord Shaftesbury, became a close friend of Spurgeon and especially supported him when he suffered from depression and, later, from rheumatic gout and Bright's disease. He wrote him the following letter of encouragement, together with a book entitled *The Psalms, with Scripture illustrations* as he was about to take some sick leave in his favourite overseas haunt, Mentone, in the south of France:

30 November, 1883
My Dear Friend,
God be with you to Mentone, at Mentone, and back again, and may he give you all the health you seek for his service!
Well may you be 'weary, and worn, and sad'. The open, avowed, boasted, modern infidelity is terrible, but the almost universality of the Laodicean spirit [the church at Laodicea was the one the risen Christ accused of being 'lukewarm – neither hot nor cold', and about whom he warned, 'I am about to spit you out of my mouth' (Revelation 2:16, NIV)] is still

4

worse. You will come back and find that socialism, contemptuous unbelief, and an utter disregard of anything but that which tends to make this world the 'be-all' and the 'end-all' of our existence, have attained vastly increased proportions during your absence.

There is nothing for it but to preach 'Jesus Christ and him crucified', with perpetual exhortation to his people to pray for his speedy return. Such a preaching of Christ has been your main strength. May God keep you in that frame of mind!

    Yours very truly,
      Shaftesbury.

Spurgeon was converted at the age of fifteen in the unlikely setting of a Primitive Methodist Chapel, where some fifteen people had braved the snow. No one knows the name of the inexperienced preacher who stood in for the regular preacher, who was snowbound. Spurgeon wrote of this day:

That happy day, when I found the Saviour, and learned to cling to his dear feet, was a day never to be forgotten by me. An obscure child, unknown, unheard of, I listened to the word of God; and that precious text, 'Look unto me, and be ye saved, all the ends of the earth,' let me see the cross of Christ . . . When I look back upon it, I can see one reason why the word was blessed to me as I heard it preached in that Primitive Methodist Chapel at Colchester (Essex); I had been up early crying to God for the blessing. As a lad, when I was seeking the Saviour, I used to rise with the sun, that I might get time to read gracious books, and to seek the Lord. I can recall the kind of pleas I used when I took my arguments, and came before the throne of grace: 'Lord, save me; it will glorify thy grace to save such a sinner as I am! Lord, save me, else I am lost to all eternity; do not let me perish, Lord! Save me, O Lord, for Jesus died! By his agony and bloody sweat, by his cross and passion, save me!'

The year after his conversion, Spurgeon became a village preacher and pastor of Waterbeach Baptist Church, Cambridgeshire. His fame as a preacher quickly spread and he was appointed as pastor of New Park Street Baptist Church in south London at the age of nineteen. Some were critical of his youth, his humour, and his lack of formal education. But Spurgeon caused such a sensation that the church had to be enlarged within one year of his arrival, in order to accommodate all the people who crowded in. On 19 October, 1856, Spurgeon took the bold step of preaching in the Surrey Gardens Music Hall, where 10,000 packed in to hear him. Even though a false fire alarm was raised on the first night that Spurgeon preached there, resulting in seven people being trampled to death, Spurgeon continued to use this centre of worldly entertainment to preach in. In 1861, Spurgeon and his congregation moved to a specially built church, the Metropolitan Tabernacle, which seated 3,600, with another 2,000 people squeezed in around the building.

When Spurgeon arrived in London in 1854 there were 232 church members, and by 1891 there were over 5,000. During this time 14,460 people had been baptized and had joined the church. During his lifetime 2,241 of his weekly sermons were published, and more than a thousand in addition during the next quarter century, bringing the total sermon circulation to over 100,000,000 worldwide, including translations into twenty-three different languages. It was not without justification that Spurgeon became known as 'the prince of preachers'.

Spurgeon was also instrumental in founding, financing (through the sales of his sermons), and supporting a Pastors' College, which trained nearly 900 men for the Baptist ministry in his lifetime (and continues to this day as Spurgeons's College); a colportage association which supported 96 full-time workers distributing Christian literature (they made 11,822,637 visits to families between 1866 and 1891, distributing over a quarter of a million texts and Scriptures in one year); and an orphanage which looked after 1,600 boys and girls during his lifetime. His wife wrote:

During the period that these various institutions were growing and flourishing, the Tabernacle Church, the foster-mother of them all, was prospering beyond all precedent. At the time of Mr Spurgeon's home-call, the number of members on the church roll was 5,311, and 22 mission stations, and 27 Sunday and Ragged School, with 612 preachers, and 8,034 scholars (comparing this great host with the little company of anxious but praying people to whom 'the boy-preacher' delivered his first discourse, in New Park Street Chapel, on that historic morning, in December, 1853 one can only say, as he said, times without number, when speaking of the blessing which the Lord had graciously vouchsafed to his ministry – WHAT HATH GOD WROUGHT![2]

Spurgeon's voluminous writings – he wrote 135 books – reveal his indebtedness to the seventeenth-century Puritans. The present volume reflects something of the variety of his writing, drawing on his poetry, hymn-writing, personal Christian experiences, devotional writings, sermons and commentaries. Included in this anthology are extracts from *The Treasury of David*, which originally ran to 5,000 pages in seven volumes and is still a much-loved exposition of all 150 Psalms. Also included are some of Spurgeon's sermons which were collected in a massive four-volume work entitled *The Treasury of the New Testament*. Thanks to the collection of letters that his wife made after his death, this present book contains a number of letters from Spurgeon which are rarely published, but which reveal a great deal about his pastoral heart. As well as records of his own remarkable conversion, told in his own words, this anthology devotes a chapter to some of the memorable conversions which Spurgeon himself recorded and which took place under his own preaching ministry. Spurgeon is especially looked to by generations of would-be evangelists, preachers and teachers of the Christian faith. So two of the lectures from his *Lectures to my Students* are included in this volume, as well as selections from his *Commenting and Commentaries* (which discloses Spurgeon's own favourite Bible commentators), his vivid illustrations from *Sermons in Candles* and selections from his short, heart-warming, devotional, daily readings entitled *The Cheque Book of the Bank of Faith*.

Through this compilation of Spurgeon's writings we recapture his deep conviction about the Bible being the Word of God for the contemporary world, his passion that Jesus Christ is the only Saviour, and his constant concern that all Christians should be edified and instructed with the teachings of the Bible.

Robert Backhouse
Norfolk 1995

Notes
1. C. H. Spurgeon, *Psalms* (Crossway Classic Commentaries). Illinois: Crossway Books, 1994, vol.1, p.xi.
2. *C. H. Spurgeon's Autobiography, compiled from his diary, letters and records.* Vol. iv. London: Passmore and Alabaster, 1900, p.278.

The Treasury of David

Psalm 19

1. *The heavens declare the glory of God.* The book of nature has three leaves: heaven, earth, and sea – of which heaven is the first and the most glorious, and by its aid we are able to see the beauties of the other two. Any book without its first page would be sadly imperfect, and especially the great Natural Bible, since its first pages, the sun, moon, and stars, supply light to the rest of the volume. Man walking erect was evidently made to scan the skies, and he who begins to read creation by studying the stars begins the book at the right place.

The *heavens* are plural for their variety, comprising the watery heavens with their clouds of countless forms, the aerial heavens with their calms and tempests, the solar heavens with all the glories of the day, and the starry heavens with all the marvels of the night; what the Heaven of heavens must be hath not entered into the heart of man, but there in chief all things are telling the glory of God. Any part of creation has more instruction in it than the human mind will ever exhaust, but the celestial realm is particularly rich in spiritual lore. The heavens *declare*, or 'are declaring', for the continuance of their testimony is intended by the participles employed; every moment God's existence, power, wisdom, and goodness are being sounded abroad by the heavenly heralds which shine upon us from above. He who would guess at divine sublimity should gaze upward into the starry vault; he who would imagine infinity must peer into the boundless expanse; he who desires to know divine fidelity must mark the regularity of the planetary motions; and he who would attain some conceptions of divine power, greatness, and majesty must estimate the forces of attraction, the magnitude of the fixed stars, and the brightness of the whole celestial train. It is not merely glory that the heavens declare, but *the glory of God*, for they deliver to us such unanswerable arguments for a conscious, planning, controlling, and presiding Creator, that no unprejudiced person can remain unconvinced by them. The testimony given by the heavens is no mere hint, but a plain, unmistakable declaration; and it is a declaration of the most constant and abiding kind. Yet for all this, to what avail is the clearest showing to one spiritually blind? God the Holy Spirit must illuminate us, or all the suns in the Milky Way never will. *The firmament sheweth his handiwork*. Not 'handy' in the popular use of that term but hand-work. The expanse is full of the works of the Lord's skillful, creating hands; hands being attributed to the great creating Spirit to set out his care and workman-like action, and to meet the poor comprehension of mortals. In the expanse above us God flies, as it were, his starry flag to show that the King is at home, that atheists may see how he despises their denunciations of him. He who looks up to the firmament and then writes himself down an atheist brands himself at the same moment as an idiot or a liar. It is strange that some who love God are yet afraid to study the God-declaring book of nature. The wisest are those who with pious eagerness trace the going forth of Jehovah as well in creation as in grace.

2. *Day unto day uttereth speech, and night unto night sheweth knowledge*. As if one took up the story where the other left it, and each night passed over the wondrous tale to the next. The original has in it the thought of pouring out, or welling over, with speech. Oh to drink often at the celestial well, and learn to utter the glory of

God! Even the changes of alternating night and day are mutely eloquent, and light and shade equally reveal the Invisible One; let the vicissitudes of our circumstances do the same, and while we bless the God of our days of joy, let us also extol him who giveth 'songs in the night'.

The lesson of day and night is one which it would be well for everyone to learn. It should be among our day-thoughts and night-thoughts to remember the flight of time, the changeful character of earthly things, the brevity both of joy and sorrow, the preciousness of life, our utter powerlessness to recall the hours once flown, and the irresistible approach of eternity. Day bids us labour, night reminds us to prepare for our last home; day bids us work for God, and night invites us to rest in him; day bids us look for endless day, and night warns us to escape from everlasting night.

3. *There is no speech nor language, where their voice is not heard.* Everyone may hear the voices of the stars. Many are the languages of terrestrials, but to celestials there is but one, and that one may be understood by every willing mind. The lowest heathen are without excuse if they do not discover the invisible things of God in the works which he has made. Sun, moon, and stars are God's travelling preachers.

4. *Their line is gone out through all the earth, and their words to the end of the world. In them hath he set a tabernacle for the sun.* Although the heavenly bodies move in solemn silence, yet in reason's ear they utter precious teachings. They give out no literal words, yet their instruction is clear enough to be so described. Nature's words are like the signs of the deaf and dumb, but grace tells us plainly of the Father. By *their line* is probably meant the measure of their domain which, together with their testimony, has gone out to the utmost end of the habitable earth. It is easy to escape from the light of ministers, but even then men with a conscience unseared will find a Nathan to accuse them, a Jonah to warn them, and an Elijah to threaten them in the silent stars of night. To gracious souls the voices of the heavens are more influential far; they are drawn towards their Father God by the bright bands of Orion.

5. *Which is as a bridegroom coming out his chamber, and rejoiceth as a strong man to run a race.* A bridegroom comes out dressed sumptuously, his face beaming with a joy which he imparts to all around; such, but with a mighty emphasis, is the rising Sun. As a champion addresses himself to the race, so does the sun speed onward with matchless regularity and unwearying swiftness in his orbit. There are no signs of effort, flagging, or exhaustion. No other creature yields such joy to the earth; but all his glory is but the glory of God.

6. *His going forth is from the end of the heaven, and his circuit unto the ends of it: and there is nothing hid from the heat thereof.* He bears his light to the boundaries of the solar heavens, denying his light to none within his range. The bowels of the earth are stored with the ancient produce of the solar rays, and even now the earth's inmost caverns feel their power. Where light is shut out, yet heat and other more subtle influences find their way.

There is no doubt a parallel intended to be drawn between the heaven of grace and the heaven of nature. God's way of grace is sublime and broad, and full of his glory; in all its displays it is to be admired and studied with diligence; both its lights and its shades are instructive; it has been proclaimed, in a measure, to every people, and in due time will be yet more completely published to the ends of the earth. Jesus, like a sun, dwells in the midst of revelation, tabernacling among men in all his brightness; rejoicing, as the Bridegroom of his church, to reveal himself to men; and, like a champion, to win to himself renown. He makes a circuit of mercy, blessing the remotest corners of the earth; and there are no seeking souls, however degraded and depraved, who will be denied the comfortable warmth and benediction of his love – even death will feel the power of his presence, and resign the bodies of the saints, and this fallen earth will be restored to its pristine glory.

7–11. In these verses we have six descriptive titles of the word, six characteristics qualities mentioned, and six divine effects declared.

7. *The law of the LORD is perfect.* He means not merely the law of Moses, but the doctrine of God, the whole run and rule of sacred

Writ. The Gospel is a complete scheme or law of gracious salvation, presenting to the needy sinner everything that his terrible necessities can possibly demand. There are no redundancies and no omissions in the Word of God, and in the plan of grace; why then do people try to paint this lily?

Converting the soul. Making people to be returned or restored to the place from which sin had cast them. The practical effect of the word of God is to turn people to themselves, to their God, and to holiness; and the turn of conversion is not outward alone – the soul is moved and renewed. The great means of the conversion of sinners is the Word of God, and the more closely we keep to it in our ministry the more likely are we to be successful. It is God's Word rather than man's comment on God's Word which is made mighty with souls. When the law drives and the Gospel draws, the action if different but the end is one, for by God's Spirit the soul is made to yield, and cries, 'Turn me, and I shall be turned'.

The testimony of the Lord is sure. God bears his testimony against sin, and on behalf of righteousness; he testifies of our fall and of our restoration; this testimony is plain, decided, and infallible, and is to be accepted as sure. God's witness in his Word is so sure that we may draw solid comfort from it both for time and eternity, and so sure that no attacks made upon it, however fierce or subtle, can ever weaken its force. What a blessing that in a world of uncertainties we have something sure to rest upon! We hasten from the quicksands of human speculations to the solid ground of divine revelation. *Making wise the simple*. Humble, candid, teachable minds receive the Word, and are made wise unto salvation. Things hidden from the wise and prudent are revealed unto babes. The persuadable grow wise, but the cavillers continue fools. As a law or plan the Word of God converts, and then as a testimony it instructs; it is not enough for us to be converts, we must continue to be disciples; and if we have felt the power of truth, we must go on to prove its certainty by experience.

8. *The statutes of the LORD are right, rejoicing the heart: the commandment of the LORD is pure, enlightening the eyes*. His precepts

and decrees are founded in righteousness, and are such as are right or fitted to the right reason of man. As a physician gives the right medicine, and a counsellor the right advice, so does God's book. Note the progress: he who was converted was next made wise and is now made happy; that truth which makes the heart right then gives joy to the right heart. Free grace brings heart-joy. No error defiles the Lord's commandment; no stain of sin pollutes it; it is the unadulterated milk, the undiluted wine. By its own purity it purges away the earthly grossness which mars the intellectual discernment; whether the eye be dim with sorrow or with sin, the Scripture is a skillful oculist, and makes the eye clear and bright. Look at the sun and it puts out your eyes; look at the more than sunlight of revelation and it enlightens them. It is well again to observe the gradation: the convert became a disciple and next a rejoicing soul; he now obtains a discerning eye, and as a spiritual person discerns all things, though he himself is discerned by no one.

9. *The fear of the LORD is clean.* The doctrine of truth is here described by its spiritual effect, namely, inward piety or the fear of the Lord; this is clean in itself, and cleanses out the love of sin, sanctifying the heart in which it reigns. Mr Godly-fear is never satisfied till every street, lane, and alley, yea, and every house and every corner of the town of Mansoul is clean rid of the Diabolonians who lurk there.

Enduring for ever. Filth brings decay, but cleanness is the great foe of corruption. The grace of God in the heart being a pure principle is also an abiding and incorruptible principle, which may be crushed for a time, but cannot be utterly destroyed. Both in the Word and in the heart, when the Lord writes, he says with Pilate, 'What I have written, I have written'. He will make no erasures himself, much less allow others to do so. The revealed will of God is never changed; even Jesus came not to destroy but to fulfil, and even the ceremonial law was only changed as to its shadow; the substance intended by it is eternal. When the governments of nations are shaken with revolution, and ancient constitutions are being repealed, it is comforting to know that the throne of God is unshaken, and his law unaltered.

The judgements of the LORD are true and righteous altogether. The Words of the Lord are true; that which is good in detail is excellent in the mass; no exception may be taken to a single clause separately, or to the book as a whole. God's judgements need no laborious excuses to justify them. They commend themselves to every truthful mind; not only is their power invincible, but their justice is unimpeachable.

10. *More to be desired are they than gold, yea, than much fine gold*. Bible truth is enriching to the soul in the highest degree; the metaphor is one which gathers force as it is brought out; gold – fine gold – much fine gold; it is good, better, best, and therefore it is not only to be desired with a miser's avidity, but with more than that. As spiritual treasure is more noble than mere material wealth, so should it be desired and sought after with greater eagerness.

Sweeter also than honey and the honeycomb. The pleasures arising from a right understanding of the divine testimonies are of the most delightful order; earthly enjoyments are utterly contemptible, if compared with them. The sweetest joys, yea, the sweetest of the sweetest falls to his portion who has God's truth to be his heritage.

11. *Moreover by them is thy servant warned*. We are warned by the Word about our duty and about our danger and about our remedy. On the sea of life there would be many more wrecks if it were not for the divine storm-signals which give to the watchful a timely warning. The Bible should be our mentor, our monitor, our remembrancer, and the keeper of our conscience.

In keeping of them there is great reward. Servants of God not only find his service delightful in itself, but they receive good recompense. Though we earn no wages of debt, we win great wages of grace. However, the main reward is yet to come, and the word here used hints at much, for it signifies the 'heel', as if the reward would come to us at the end of life when the work was done; not while the labour was in the hand, but when it was done and we could see the heel of it. Oh the glory yet to be revealed!

12. *Who can understand his errors?* A question which is its own answer. It requires an exclamation point rather than a question mark. By the law is the knowledge of sin, and in the presence of divine truth the psalmist marvels at the number and heinousness of his sins. He best knows himself who best knows the Word of God, but even such a person will be in a maze of wonder as to what he does not know. Augustine wrote in his older days a series of Retractations; ours might make a library if we had enough grace to be convinced of our mistakes and to confess them.

Cleanse thou me from secret faults. Thou canst mark in me faults entirely hidden from myself. It is hopeless to expect me to see all my spots; therefore, O Lord, wash away in the atoning blood even those sins which my conscience has been unable to detect. Secret sins, like private conspirators, must be hunted out, or they may do deadly mischief; it is well to be much in prayer concerning them. If we had eyes like those of God, we would think very differently of ourselves.

13. *Keep back thy servant also from presumptuous sins; let them not have dominion over us.* This earnest and humble prayer teaches us that saints may fall into the worst of sins unless restrained by grace, and that therefore they must watch and pray lest they enter into temptation. There is a natural proneness to sin in the best of men, and they must be held back as a horse is held back by the bit or they will run into it. Presumptuous sins are particularly dangerous. All sins are great sins, but yet some sins are greater than others. Every sin has in it the very venom of rebellion; but there are some sins which have in them a greater development of the essential mischief of rebellion, and which wear upon their faces more of the brazen pride which defies the Most High. It is wrong to suppose that because all sins will condemn us, that therefore one sin is not greater than another. The presumptuous sins of our text are the chief and worst of all sins. It is remarkable that though an atonement was provided under the Jewish law for every kind of sin, there was this one exception: 'But the soul that sinneth presumptuously shall have no atonement; it shall be cut off from the midst of my

16

people.' And now under the Christian dispensation, although in the sacrifice of our blessed Lord there is a great and precious atonement for presumptuous sins, whereby sinners who have erred in this manner are made clean, yet without doubt presumptuous sinners, dying without pardon, must expect to receive a double portion of the wrath of God. For this reason is David so anxious that he may never come under the reigning power of these giant evils.

Then shall I be upright, and I shall be innocent from the great transgression. He shudders at the thought of the unpardonable sin. Secret sin is a stepping-stone to presumptuous sin, and that is the vestibule of 'the sin which is unto death'. He who is not wilful in his sin will be in a fair way to be innocent so far as poor sinful man can be; but he who tempts the devil to tempt him is in a path which will lead him from bad to worse, and from the worse to the worst.

14. *Let the words of my mouth, and the meditation of my heart, be acceptable in thy sight, O LORD, my strength, and my redeemer.* A sweet prayer, and so spiritual that it is almost as commonly used in Christian worship as the apostolic benediction. Words are a mockery if the heart does not meditate; but both together are useless unless accepted; and even if accepted by man, it is all vanity if not acceptable in the sight of God. We must in prayer view Jehovah as our strength enabling, and our Redeemer saving, or we shall not pray aright, and it is well to feel our personal interest so as to use the word 'my', or our prayers will be hindered. Blessed Redeemer, give us now to meditate acceptably upon thy most sweet love and tenderness.

Psalm 22

1. *My God, my God, why hast thou forsaken me?* This was the startling cry of Golgotha: 'Eloi, Eloi, lama sabacthani'. The Jews mocked, but the angels adored when Jesus cried this exceedingly bitter cry. Nailed to the tree we behold our great Redeemer in

extremities, and what do we see? Let us gaze with holy wonder, and mark the flashes of light amid the awful darkness of that midday-midnight. First, our Lord's faith deserves our reverent imitation; he keeps his hold upon his God and cries twice, 'My God, my God'. The spirit of adoption was strong within the suffering Son of Man, and he felt no doubt about his interest in his God. Oh that we could imitate this cleaving to an afflicting God! Nor does the sufferer distrust the power of God to sustain him, for the title used – 'El' – signifies strength, and is the name of the Mighty God. He knows the Lord to be the all-sufficient support and succour of his spirit, and therefore appeals to him in the agony of grief, but not in the misery of doubt. He would like to know why he is left; he raises that question and repeats it, but neither the power nor the faithfulness of God does he mistrust. What an enquiry is this before us?

Why has thou forsaken me? We must lay the emphasis on every word of this saddest of all utterances.

Why? There was no cause in him; why then was he deserted?

Hast. It is done, and the Saviour is feeling its dread effect; it is surely true, but how mysterious! It was no threatening of forsaking which made the great Surety cry aloud: he endured that forsaking in every deed.

Thou. I can understand why traitorous Judas and timid Peter should be gone, but *thou*, my God, my faithful friend, how canst thou leave me? This is worst of all, worse than all put together. Hell itself has for its fiercest flame the separation of the soul from God.

Forsaken. If thou hadst chastened I might bear it, for thy face would shine; but to forsake me utterly, ah! why is this?

Me. Thine innocent, obedient, suffering Son, why leavest thou *me* to perish? A sight of self seen by penitence, and of Jesus on the cross seen by faith will best expound this question. Jesus is forsaken because our sins had separated between us and God.

Why art thou so far from helping me, and from the words of my roaring? The Man of Sorrows had prayed until his speech failed him, and he could only utter moanings and groanings as men do in severe sicknesses, like the roarings of a wounded animal. To what extremity of grief was our Master driven! What a strong crying and tears were those which made him too hoarse for speech! What must have been his anguish to find his own beloved and trusted Father standing afar off, and neither granting help nor apparently hearing prayer! Yet there was a reason for all this which those who rest in Jesus as their Substitute will know.

2. *O my God, I cry in the daytime, but thou hearest not; and in the night season, and am not silent.* For our prayer to appear to be unheard is no new trial. Jesus felt it before us. He still held fast on God, and cried still, 'My God,' but his faith did not render him less importunate. Our Lord continued to pray even though no comfortable answer came, and in this he set us an example of obedience to the words, 'men ought always to pray, and not to faint'. No daylight is too glaring and no midnight too dark to pray in; no delay or apparent denial, however grievous, should tempt us to forbear from importunate pleading.

3. *But thou art holy, O thou that inhabitest the praises of Israel.* However ill things may look there is no ill in thee, O God! We are very apt to think and speak hardly of God when we are under his affecting hand, but not so the obedient Son. He knows too well his Father's goodness to let outward circumstances libel his character. There is no unrighteousness with the God of Jacob. If prayer be unanswered it is not because God is unfaithful. If we cannot perceive any ground for the delay, we must leave the riddle unsolved, but we must not fly in God's face to invent an answer. While the holiness of God is acknowledged and adored, the afflicted speaker in this verse seems to marvel at how the holy God could forsake him, and be silent to his cries. The argument is: Thou art holy; oh, why is it that thou dost disregard thy holy One in his hour of sharpest anguish? We may not question the holiness of God, but we may argue from it, and use it as a plea in our petitions.

4. *Our fathers trusted in thee: they trusted, and thou didst deliver them.* This is the rule of life with all the chosen family. Three times over is it mentioned that they trusted; they never left off trusting, for it was their very life; and they fared well, too, for *thou didst*

deliver them. Out of all their straits, difficulties, and miseries faith brought them by calling their God to the rescue; but in the case of our Lord it appeared as if faith would bring no assistance from heaven; he alone of all the trusting ones was to remain without deliverance. The experience of other saints may be a great consolation to us when in deep waters, if faith can be sure that their deliverance will be ours; but when we feel ourselves sinking, it is poor comfort to know that others are swimming. Our Lord here pleads the past dealings of God with his people as a reason why he should not be left alone; here again he is an example to us in the skillful use of the weapon of all prayer. The use of the plural pronoun *our* shows how one with his people Jesu was even on the cross. We say, 'Our Father which art in heaven,' and he calls those 'our fathers' through whom we came into the world, although he was without father as to the flesh.

5. *They cried unto thee, and were delivered: they trusted in thee, and were not confounded*. As if he had said, 'How is it that I am now left without succour in my overwhelming griefs, while all others have been helped?' We may remind the Lord of his former lovingkindnesses to his people, and beseech him to be still the same. This is true wrestling; let us learn the art. Observe that ancient saints *cried* and *trusted*, and that in times of trouble we must do the same; and the invariable result was that they were not ashamed of their hope, for deliverance came in due time; this same happy portion will be ours. The prayer of faith can do the deed when nothing else can. Let us wonder when we see Jesus using the same pleas as ourselves, and immersed in grief far deeper than our own.

6. *But I am a worm, and no man*. How could the Lord of glory be brought to such abasement as to be not only lower than the angels, but even lower than men? What a contrast between 'I AM' and *I am a worm*! Yet such a double nature was found in the person of our Lord Jesus when bleeding on the tree. He felt himself to be comparable to a helpless, powerless, downtrodden worm, passive while crushed, and unnoticed and despised by those who trod on him. He selects the weakest of creatures, which is all flesh; and becomes,

when trodden upon, writhing, quivering flesh, utterly devoid of any might except strength to suffer. This was a true likeness of himself when his body and soul had become a mass of misery – the very essence of agony – in the dying pangs of crucifixion. Man by nature is but a worm; but our Lord puts himself even beneath man, on account of the scorn which was heaped upon him and the weakness which he felt, and therefore he adds *and no man*. The privileges and blessings which belonged to the fathers he could not obtain while deserted by God, and common acts of humanity were not allowed him, for he was rejected of men; he was outlawed from the society of earth, and shut out from the smile of heaven. How utterly did the Saviour empty himself of all glory, and become of no reputation for our sakes!

A reproach of men. Their common butt and jest; a byword and a proverb unto them; the sport of the rabble, and the scorn of the rulers. Oh the caustic power of reproach, to those who endure it with patience, yet smart under it most painfully!

And despised of the people. The very people who would once have crowned him then condemned him, and they who were benefited by his cures sneered at him in his woes. Sin was worthy of all reproach and contempt, and for this reason Jesus, the Sinbearer, was given up to be thus unworthily and shamefully entreated.

7. *All they that see me laugh me to scorn: they shoot out the lip, they shake the head.* Read the evangelistic narrative of the ridicule endured by the Crucified One, and then consider how it grieved him. The iron entered into his soul. The scornful ridicule of our Lord was unanimous. Which shall we wonder at the most, the cruelty of man or the love of the bleeding Saviour? How can we ever complain of ridicule after this? Pouting, grinning, shaking of the head, thrusting out of the tongue, and other modes of derision were endured by our patient Lord; men made faces at him before whom angels veil their faces and adore. They punned upon his prayer; they made matter for laughter of his sufferings, and set him utterly at nought.

8. *He trusted on the* LORD *that he would deliver him: let him*

deliver him, seeing he delighted in him. Here the taunt is cruelly aimed at the sufferer's faith in God, which is the tenderest point in a good man's soul, the very apple of his eye. They must have learned the art from Satan himself, for they made rare proficiency in it. There were five forms of taunt hurled at the Lord Jesus (Matthew 27:39–44); this mockery is probably mentioned in this psalm because it is the most bitter of the whole. When we are tormented in the same manner, let us remember him who endured such contradiction of sinners against himself. We must not lose sight of the truth which was unwittingly uttered by the Jewish scoffers. They themselves are witnesses that Jesus of Nazareth trusted in God: why then was he permitted to perish? Jehovah had previously delivered those who rolled their burdens upon him; why was this man deserted? Of that they had understood the answer! Their principal jest, *seeing he delighted in him*, was true. The Lord did delight in his dear Son, and when he became obedient unto death, he still was well pleased in him. Jehovah delights in him, and yet slays him.

9. *Thou art he that took me out of the womb*. Kindly providence attends with the surgery of tenderness at every human birth; but the Son of Man, who was marvellously begotten of the Holy Spirit, was in an especial manner watched over by the Lord when brought forth by Mary. The destitute state of Joseph and Mary, far away from friends and home, led them to see the cherishing hand of God in the safe delivery of the mother. Her child, now fighting the great battle of his life, uses the mercy of his nativity as an argument with God. Faith finds weapons everywhere. The person who desires to believe will never lack reasons for believing.

Thou didst make me hope when I was upon my mother's breasts. Was our Lord one of those babes and sucklings out of whose mouths strength is ordained? Early piety gives particular comfort in our later trials, for surely he who loved us when we were children is too faithful to cast us off in our riper years. Some give the text the sense of 'gave me cause to trust, by keeping me safely', and assuredly there was a special providence which preserved our Lord's infant

22

days from the fury of Herod, the dangers of travelling, and the ills of poverty.

10. *I was cast upon thee from the womb.* Into the Almighty arms he was first received, as into those of a loving parent. God begins his care over us from the earliest hour.

Thou art my God from my mother's belly. The psalm begins with 'My God, my God,' and here not only is the claim repeated but its early date is urged. Our birth was our weakest and most perilous period of existence; if we were then secured by omnipotent tenderness, surely we have no cause to suspect that divine goodness will fail us now.

11. *Be not far from me.* This is the petition for which he has been using such varied and powerful pleas. His great woe was that God had forsaken him; his great prayer is that he would be near him. A lively sense of the divine presence is a mighty stay to the heart in times of distress.

For trouble is near; for there is none to help. There are two *for*, as though faith gave a double knock at mercy's gate; that is a powerful prayer which is full of holy reasons and thoughtful arguments. The nearness of trouble is a weighty motive for divine help; this moves our heavenly Father's heart, and brings down his helping hand. It is his glory to be our very present help in trouble. Our Substitute had trouble in his inmost heart, for he said, 'the waters have come in, even unto my soul'; well might he cry, *be not far from me.* The absence of all other helpers is another telling plea. In our Lord's case none either could or would help him; yet it was a sore aggravation to find that all his disciples had forsaken him, and lover and friend were put far from him. There is an awfulness about absolute friendlessness which is crushing to the human mind, for man was not made to be alone, and is like a dismembered limb when he has to endure heart-loneliness.

12. *Many bulls have compassed me: strong bulls of Bashan have beset me round.* The mighty ones in the crowd are here marked by the tearful eye of their victim. The priests, elders, scribes, Pharisees, rulers, and captains bellowed round the cross like wild

cattle, full of strength and fury. The Rejected One was all alone, and bound naked to the tree.

13. *They gaped upon me with their mouths, as a ravening and a roaring lion*. Like hungry cannibals they opened their blasphemous mouths as if they were about to swallow the man whom they abhorred. They could not commit forth their anger fast enough, and therefore set the doors of their lips wide open like those who gape. Our Lord's faith must have passed through a most severe conflict while he found himself abandoned to the tender mercies of the wicked, but he came off victorious by prayer, the very danger to which he was exposed being used to add prevalence to his entreaties.

14. Turning from his enemies, our Lord describes his own personal condition in language which should bring the tears into every loving eye.

I am poured out like water. He was utterly spent, like water poured upon the earth; his heart failed him, and had no more firmness in it than running water, and his whole being was made a sacrifice, like a libation poured out before the Lord. He had long been a fountain of tears; in Gethsemane his heart welled over in sweat, so that he was reduced to the most feeble and exhausted state.

All my bones are out of joint. As if distended upon a rack. Is it not most probable that the fastening of the hands and feet, and the jar occasioned by fixing the cross in the earth, may have dislocated the bones of the Crucified One? If this is not intended, we must refer the expression to that extreme weakness which would occasion relaxation of the muscles and a general sense of parting asunder throughout the whole system

My heart is like wax; it is melted in the midst of my bowels. Excessive debility and intense pain made his inmost life to feel like wax melted in the heat. The Greek liturgy uses the expression 'thine unknown sufferings', and well it may. The fire of almighty wrath would have consumed our souls for ever in hell; it was no light work to bear as a substitute the heat of an anger so justly terrible.

15. *My strength is dried up like a potsherd; and my tongue cleaveth to my jaws; and thou hast brought me into the dust of death*. Most complete disability is here portrayed; Jesus likens himself to a broken piece of earthenware, or an earthen pot, baked in the fire till the last particle of moisture is driven out of the clay. No doubt a high degree of feverish burning afflicted the body of our Lord. All his strength was dried up in the tremendous flames of avenging justice, just as the paschal lamb was roasted in the fire. Thirst and fever fastened his tongue to his jaws, so that he could scarcely speak. So tormented in every single part as to feel dissolved into separate atoms, and each atom full of misery, the full price of our redemption was paid, and no part of the Surety's body or soul escaped its share of agony. The Lord of Glory stoops to the dust of death.

16. We are to understand every item of this sad description as being urged by the Lord Jesus as a plea for divine help; and this will give us a high idea of his perseverance in prayer.

For dogs have compassed me. Here he marks the more ignoble crowd, who were howling like hungry dogs. Hunters frequently surround their game with a circle, and gradually encompass them with an ever-narrowing ring of dogs and men. Such a picture is before us. In the centre stands, not a panting stag, but a bleeding, fainting man, and around him are the enraged and unpitying wretches who have hounded him to his doom. Here we have the 'hind of the morning' of whom the psalm so plaintively sings, hunted by bloodhounds, all thirsting to devour him.

The assembly of the wicked have enclosed me. Thus the Jewish people, which called itself an assembly of the righteous, is justly for its sins marked upon the forehead as an assembly of the wicked. This is not the only occasion when professed churches of God have become synagogues of Satan, and have persecuted the Holy One and the Just.

They pierced my hands and my feet. This can by no means refer to David, or to anyone but Jesus of Nazareth. Pause, and view the wounds of the Redeemer.

17. So emaciated was Jesus by his fastings and suffering that he says, *I may tell all my bones*. He could count and re-count them. The zeal of his Father's house had eaten him up. Oh that we cared less for the body's enjoyment and ease and more for our Father's business! It is better to count the bones of an emaciated body than to bring leanness into our souls.

They look and stare upon me. Unholy eyes gazed insultingly upon the Saviour's nakedness. The sight of the agonizing body ought to have ensured sympathy from the throng, but it only increased their savage mirth as they gloated over our Redeemer's shame. The first Adam made us all naked, and therefore the second Adam became naked that he might clothe our naked souls.

18. *They part my garments among them, and cast lots upon my vesture*. The garments of the executed were the perquisites of the executioners in most cases, but it was not often that they cast lots at the division of the spoil; this incident shows how clearly David in vision saw the day of Christ, and how surely the Man of Nazareth is he of whom the prophets spoke. It may be noted that the habit of gambling is of all others the most hardening, for men could prac- tise it even at the cross-foot while besprinkled with the blood of the Crucified. No Christian will endure the rattle of the dice when he thinks of this.

19. *But be not thou far from me, O God*. Invincible faith returns to the charge, and uses the same means, namely, importunate prayer. He repeats the petition offered before. He wants nothing but his God, even in his lowest state. He does not ask for the most comfort- able or nearest presence of God; he will be content if he is not far from him; humble requests speed at the throne.

O my strength, haste thee to help me. Hard cases need timely aid; when necessity justifies it we may be urgent with God as to time, but we must not do this out of wilfulness. In the last degree of weakness he calls the Lord *my strength*; after this fashion the believer can sing, 'when I am weak, then am I strong'.

20. *Deliver my soul from the sword*. By *the sword* is probably meant entire destruction, which as a man he dreaded; or perhaps he

26

sought deliverance from the enemies around him, who were like a sharp and deadly sword to him. The Lord had said, 'Awake, O sword', and now from the terror of that sword the Shepherd wanted to be delivered as soon as justice should see fit.

My darling from the power of the dog. Meaning his soul, his life, which is most dear to every person. The origin is, 'my only one', and therefore is our soul dear, because it is our only soul. Would that everyone made their souls their darlings, but many treat them as if they were not worth so much as the mire of the streets. The *dog* may mean Satan, or else the whole company of Christ's foes, who though many in number were but one. If Jesus cried for help against the dog of hell, much more may we. Beware of the dog, for his power is great, and only God can deliver us from him. When he fawns upon us, we must not put ourselves in his power; and when he howls at us, we may remember that God holds him with a chain.

21. *Save me from the lion's mouth: for thou hast heard me from the horns of the unicorns.* Having experienced deliverance in the past from our great enemies, who were strong as the unicorns, the Redeemer utters his last cry for rescue from death, which is fierce and mighty as the lion. This prayer was heard, and the gloom of the cross departed. Thus faith, though sorely beaten, and even cast beneath the feet of her enemy, ultimately wins the victory. It was so in our Head; it shall be so in all the members. We have overcome the unicorn, we shall conquer the lion, and from both lion and unicorn we shall take the crown.

22–31. The transition is very marked; from a horrible tempest all is changed into calm. The darkness of Calvary at length passed away from the face of nature, and from the soul of the Redeemer, and beholding the light of his triumph and its future results the Saviour's smile. It will be well still to regard the words as a part of our Lord's soliloquy upon the cross, uttered in his mind during the last few moments before his death.

22. *I will declare thy name unto my brethren.* The delights of Jesus are always with his church, and hence his thoughts, after much distraction, return at the first moment of relief to their usual

27

channel; he forms fresh designs for the benefit of his loved one. He is not ashamed to call them brethren. He anticipates happiness in having communication with his people; he intends to be their teacher and minister, and fixes his mind upon the subject of his discourse. The name, i.e. the character and conduct of God, are by Jesus Christ's Gospel proclaimed to all the holy brotherhood; they behold the fullness of the Godhead dwelling bodily in him, and rejoice greatly to see all the infinite perfections manifested in one who is bone of their bone and flesh of their flesh. What a precious subject is the name of our God! It is the only one worthy of the only Begotten, whose meat and drink it was to do the Father's will. We may learn from this resolution of our Lord that one of the most excellent methods of showing our thankfulness for deliverances is to tell to our brethren what the Lord has done for us. We mention our sorrows readily enough; why are we so slow in declaring our deliverances?

In the midst of the congregation will I praise thee. Not in a little household gathering merely does our Lord resolve to proclaim his Father's love, but in the great assemblies of his saints, and in the general assembly and church of the first-born. This he is always doing by his representatives, who are the heralds of salvation, and labour to praise God. In the great universal church Jesus is the one authoritative teacher, and all other are nothing but echoes of his voice. Jesus declares the divine name so that God may be praised. The church continually magnifies Jehovah for revealing himself in the person of Jesus, and Jesus himself leads the song, and is both leader and preacher in his church. Delightful are the seasons when Jesus communes with our hearts concerning divine truth; joyful praises are the sure result.

23. *Ye that fear the LORD, praise him; all ye the seed of Jacob, glorify him; and fear him, all ye the seed of Israel.* Imagine the Saviour as addressing the congregation of the saints. He exhorts the faithful to unite with him in thanksgiving. The description of 'fearing the Lord' is very frequent and very instructive; it is the beginning of wisdom, and is an essential sign of grace. Humble awe

28

of God is so necessary a preparation for praising him that none are fit to sing to his honour but such as reverence his Word; but this fear is consistent with the highest joy, and is not to be confounded with legal bondage, which is a fear which perfect love casteth out. Jew and Gentile saved by sovereign grace should be eager in magnifying the God of our salvation: *all* saints should unite in the song. The spiritual Israel all *fear* him, and we hope the day will come when the bodily Israel will be brought to the same mind. The more we praise God the more reverently shall we fear him, and the sweeter will be our songs.

24. *For he hath not despised nor abhorred the affliction of the afflicted.* Here is good matter and motive for praise. The experience of our covenant Head and Representative should encourage all of us to bless the God of grace. Never was man so afflicted as our Saviour in body and soul from friends and foes, by heaven and hell, in life and death; he was the foremost in the ranks of the afflicted, but all those afflictions were sent in love, and not because his Father despised and abhorred him. It is true that justice demanded that Christ should bear the burden which as a substitute he undertook to carry, but Jehovah always loved him, and in love laid that load upon him with a view to his ultimate glory and to the accomplishment of the dearest wish of his heart. Under all his woes our Lord was honourable in the Father's sight.

Neither hath he hid his face from him. The hiding was but temporary, and was soon removed; it was not final and eternal.

But when he cried unto him, he heard. Jesus was heard in that he feared. He cried from the depths, and was speedily answered; he therefore bids his people to join him in singing a Gloria.

Every child of God should seek refreshment for his faith in this testimony of the Man of Sorrows. What Jesus here witnesses is as true today as when it was first written. It shall never be said that anyone's affliction or poverty prevented his being an accepted suppliant at Jehovah's throne of grace.

25. *My praise shall be of thee in the great congregation.* The one subject of our Master's song is the Lord alone. The word in the

original is 'from thee' – true praise is of celestial origin. The rarest harmonies of music are nothing unless they are sincerely consecrated to God by hearts sanctified by the Spirit. The cleric says, 'Let us sing to the praise and glory of God,' but the choir often sing to the praise and glory of themselves. Oh when shall our service of song be a pure offering? Observe how Jesus loves the public praises of the saints. It would be wicked on our part to despise the twos and threes; but, on the other hand, let not the little companies snarl at the greater assemblies as though they were necessarily less pure and less approved, for Jesus loves the praise of the great congregation.

I will pay my vows before them that fear him. Jesus dedicates himself anew to the carrying out of the divine purpose in fulfilment of his vows made in anguish. Did our Lord when he ascended to the skies proclaim amid the redeemed in glory the goodness of Jehovah? And was that the vow meant here? Undoubtedly the publication of the Gospel is the constant fulfilment of covenant engagements. The Messiah vowed to build up a spiritual temple for the Lord, and he will surely keep his word.

26. *The meek shall eat and be satisfied.* Mark how the dying Lover of our souls solaces himself with the result of his death. The spiritually poor find a feast in Jesus, to the satisfaction of their hearts. The thought of the joy of his people gave comfort to our expiring Lord. Note the characters who partake of the benefit of his passion: the *meek*, the humble, and lowly. Lord, make us so. Note also the certainty that Gospel provisions will not be wasted – *they shall eat* – and the sure result of such eating – *and be satisfied. They shall praise the LORD that seek him.* For a while they may keep a fast, but their thanksgiving days must and will come. *Your heart shall live for ever.* Your spirits will not fail through trial. Thus Jesus speaks even from the cross to the troubled seeker. If his dying words are so assuring, what consolation may we not find in the truth that he ever liveth to make intercession for us! Those who eat at Jesus' table receive the fulfilment of the promise, 'Whosoever eateth of this bread shall live forever'.

27. *All the ends of the world shall remember and turn unto the* LORD: *and all the kindreds of the nations shall worship before thee.* One is struck with the Messiah's missionary spirit. It is evidently his grand consolation that Jehovah will be known throughout all places of his dominion. Out from the inner circle of the present church the blessing is spread in growing power until the remotest parts of the earth will be ashamed of their idols, mindful of the true God, penitent for their offences, and unanimously earnest for reconciliation with Jehovah. Then shall false worship cease. This is a stimulus to those who fight his battles.

It is well to mark the order of conversion: they shall *remember* — this is reflection, like the prodigal who came to himself; *and turn unto Jehovah* — this is repentance, like Manasseh who left his idols; and *worship* — this is holy service, as Paul adored the Christ whom once he abhorred.

28. *For the kingdom is the* LORD's: *and he is the governor among the nations.* As an obedient Son the dying Redeemer rejoiced to know that his Father's interests would prosper through his pains. He who by his own power reigns supreme in creation and providence has set up a new kingdom of grace, and by the conquering power of the cross that kingdom will grow until all people proclaim that *he is the governor among the nations.* Amid the tumults and disasters of the present the Lord reigns; but in the halcyon days of peace the rich fruit of his dominion will be apparent to every eye.

29. *All they that be fat upon the earth.* The rich and great are not shut out. Grace now finds most of its jewels among the poor, but in the latter days the mighty of the earth *shall eat,* with all their hearts the God who deals so bountifully with us in Christ Jesus. Those who are spiritually fat with inward prosperity will be filled with the marrow of communion, and worship the Lord with especial fervour. In the covenant of grace Jesus has provided good cheer for our high estate, and taken equal care to console us in our humiliation: *all they that go down to the dust shall bow before him.* There is relief and comfort in bowing before God when our case is at its worst; even amid the dust of death prayer kindles the lamp of hope.

31

None can keep alive his own soul. While all who come to God by Jesus Christ are thus blessed, whether rich or poor, none who despise him may hope for a blessing. This is the stern counterpart of the Gospel message of 'look and live'. We must have life as Christ's gift, or we shall die eternally. This should be proclaimed in every corner of the earth, that it may break in pieces all self-confidence.

30. *A seed shall serve him; it shall be accounted to the Lord for a generation.* Posterity will perpetuate the worship of the Most High. The kingdom of truth on earth will never fail. The Lord will reckon the ages by the succession of the saints. Generations of sinners come not into the genealogy of the skies. God's family register is not for strangers, but for the children only.

31. *They shall come.* Sovereign grace will bring out from among men the blood-bought ones. Nothing will thwart the divine purpose. In this the dying Saviour finds a sacred satisfaction.

And shall declare his righteousness unto a people that shall be born. None of the people brought to God by the irresistible attractions of the cross will be dumb; they will be able to tell out the righteousness of the Lord, so that future generations know the truth. Fathers will teach their sons, who will hand it down to their children; the burden of the story always being *that he hath done this*, or, that 'It is finished'. Salvation's glorious work is done, there is peace on earth, and glory in the highest.

Psalm 23

1. *The LORD is my shepherd.* It should be the subject of grateful admiration that the great God allows himself to be compared to anything which will set forth his great love and care for his own people. David had himself been a keeper of sheep, and understood both the needs of the sheep and the many cares of a shepherd. He compares himself to a creature weak, defenceless, and foolish, and he takes God to be his Provider, Preserver, Director, and indeed his

everything. No one has a right to consider himself the Lord's sheep unless his nature has been renewed, for the scriptural description of the unconverted does not picture them as sheep but as wolves or goats. A sheep is an object of property, not a wild animal; its owner set great store by it, and frequently it is bought with a great price. It is well to know, as certainly David did, that we belong to the Lord. There is no 'if' or 'but' or even 'I hope so' in this sentence. We must cultivate the spirit of assured dependence on our heavenly Father.

The sweetest word of the whole is my. He does not say, 'The Lord is the shepherd of the world at large, and leadeth forth the multitude as his flock.' If he is a Shepherd to no one else, he is a Shepherd to *me*. The words are in the present tense. Whatever the believer's position, he is under the pastoral care of Jehovah now.

I shall not want. These positive words are a sort of inference from the first statement. When the Lord is my Shepherd he is able to supply my needs, and he is certainly willing to do so, for his heart is full of love. I shall not lack temporal things: does he not feed the ravens, and cause the lilies to grow? How then can he leave his children to starve? I shall not lack spiritual things; I know that his grace will be sufficient for me. I may not possess all that I wish for, but I shall not lack. Others may, far wealthier and wiser than I, but I shall not. 'The young lions do lack, and suffer hunger: but they that seek the Lord shall not want any good thing.' It is not only 'I do not want,' but 'I shall not want.' Come what may, if famine should devastate the land, or calamity destroy the city, 'I shall not want.' Old age with its feebleness will not bring me any lack, and even death with its gloom will not find me destitute. I have all things and abound; not because I have a good store of money in the bank, not because I have skill and wit with which to win my bread, but because *The LORD is my shepherd*. The wicked always want, but the righteous never; a sinner's heart is far from satisfaction, but a gracious spirit dwells in the place of content.

2. *He maketh me to lie down in green pastures: he leadeth me beside the still waters*. The Christian life has two elements in it, the contemplative and the active, and both are richly provided for.

What are the *green pastures* but the Scriptures of truth -- always fresh, always rich, and never exhausted? When by faith we are enabled to find rest in the promises, we are like the sheep that lie down in the pasture; we find at the same moment both rest and refreshment. It is the Lord who graciously enables us to perceive the preciousness of his truth, and to feed upon it. How grateful ought we to be for the power to appropriate the promises! There are some distracted souls who would give worlds if they could only do this. They know the blessedness of it, but they cannot say that this blessedness is theirs. Those believers who have for years enjoyed a 'full assurance of faith' should greatly bless their gracious God.

The second part of a vigorous Christian's life consists in gracious activity. We are not always lying down to feed, but are journeying onward towards perfection. What are the *still waters* but the influences and graces of his blessed Spirit? His Spirit attends us in various operations, like waters – in the plural – to cleanse, to refresh, to fertilise, to cherish. They are *still* because the Holy Spirit loves peace, and sounds no trumpet of ostentation in his operations. He may flow into our soul, but not into our neighbour's, and therefore our neighbour may not perceive the divine presence. Our Lord leads us beside these still waters; we could not go there of ourselves, we need his guidance. He does not drive us. Moses drives us by the law, but Jesus leads us by his example, and the gentle drawing of his love.

3. *He restoreth my soul*. When the soul grows sorrowful he revives it; when it is sinful he sanctifies it; when it is weak he strengthens it. *He* does it. His ministers could not do it if he did not. His Word would not avail by itself. He *restoreth*: do we feel that our spirituality is at its lowest ebb? He who turns the ebb into the flood can soon restore our soul. Pray to him, then, for the blessing.

He leadeth me in the paths of righteousness for his name's sake. The Christian delights to be obedient, but it is the obedience of love, to which he is constrained by the example of his Master. He is not obedient to some commandments and neglectful of others; he does not pick and choose, but yields to all. Observe that the plural is used – the *paths* or righteousness. Whatever God may give us to do we would do it, led by his love. Some Christians overlook the blessing of sanctification, and yet to a thoroughly renewed heart this is one of the sweetest gifts of the covenant. If we could be saved from wrath, and yet remain unregenerate, impenitent sinners, we should not be saved as we desire, for we mainly and chiefly pant to be saved from sin and led in the way of holiness. All this is done out of pure free grace, *for his name's sake*. It is to the honour of our great Shepherd that we should be a holy people, walking in the narrow way of righteousness. If we are so led and guided, we must not fail to adore our heavenly Shepherd's care.

4. *Yea, though I walk through the valley of the shadow of death, I will fear no evil: for thou art with me; thy rod and thy staff they comfort me.* This has been sung on many a dying bed, and has helped to make the dark valley bright times out of mind. Every word in it has a wealth of meaning. *Yea, though I walk*, as if the believer did not quicken his pace when he came to die, but still calmly walked with God. To walk indicates the steady advance of a soul which knows its road, knows its end, resolves to follow the path, feels quite safe, and is therefore perfectly calm and composed.

It is not walking in the valley but *through* the valley. We go through the dark tunnel of death and emerge into the light of immortality. We do not die; we only sleep, to wake in glory. Death is not the goal but the passage to it. The storm breaks on the mountain, but the valley is a place of quietude, and thus often the last days of the Christian are the most peaceful in his whole career; the mountain is bleak and bare, but the valley is rich with golden sheaves, and many a saint has reaped more joy and knowledge when he came to die than he ever knew while he lived. And, then, it is not 'the valley of death' but 'the valley of *the shadow* of death', for death in its substance has been removed, and only the shadow of it remains. Someone has said that when there is a shadow there must be light somewhere. Death stands by the side of the highway in which we have to travel, and the light of heaven shining upon him throws a shadow across our path; let us then rejoice that there is a light beyond. A shadow cannot stop a man's pathway even for a moment. Let us not, therefore, be afraid.

I will fear no evil. He does not say there will not be any evil; he had got beyond even that high assurance, and knew that Jesus had put all evil away; but his fears, those shadows of evil, were gone for ever. The worst evils of life are those which do not exist except in our imagination. We feel a thousand deaths in fearing one, but the psalmist was cured of the disease of fearing. 'I will fear no evil,' not even the Evil One himself; I will look upon him as a conquered foe, an enemy to be destroyed, *for thou art with me.* This is the joy of the Christian! The little child out at sea in the storm is not frightened like all the other passengers; it is asleep in its mother's bosom; it is enough for it that its mother is with it; and it should be enough for the believer to know that Christ is with him; *thy rod and thy staff,* by which thou governest and rulest thy flock, the ensigns of thy sovereignty and of thy gracious care, *they comfort me.*

Many people profess to receive much comfort from the hope that they will not die. Certainly there will be some who will be 'alive and remain' at the coming of the Lord, but is there so very much of advantage in such an escape from death as to make it the object of Christian desire? Those who 'shall be caught up together with the Lord in the air' will lose that actual fellowship with Christ in the tomb which dying saints will have, and we are expressly told they will have no preference beyond those who are asleep. Let us be of Paul's mind when he said that 'to die is gain', and think of 'departing to be with Christ, which is far better'. This psalm is as sweet in a believer's ear now as it was in David's time.

5. *Thou preparest a table before me in the presence of mine enemies.* The good man has his enemies. He would not be like his Lord if he had not. If we were without enemies we might fear that we were not the friends of God, for the friendship of the world is enmity to God. Yet see the quietude of the godly man in spite of, and in the sight of, his enemies. How refreshing is his calm bravery! When a soldier is in the presence of his enemies, if he eats at all he snatches

36

a hasty meal, and away he hastens to the fight. But observe: *Thou prepares a table*, just as a servant does when she unfolds the damask cloth and displays the ornaments of the feast on an ordinary peaceful occasion. Nothing is hurried, the enemy is at the door, and yet God prepares a table, and the Christian sits down and eats as if everything were in perfect peace.

Thou anointed my head with oil. May we receive a fresh anointing for every day's duties. Every Christian is a priest, but must go day by day to God the Holy Spirit. A priest without oil misses the chief qualification for his office, and the Christian priest lacks his chief fitness for service when he is devoid of new grace from on high.

My cup runneth over. He had not only enough, but more than enough. A poor man may say this as well as those in higher circumstances. A man may be ever so wealthy, but if he is discontented his cup cannot run over; it is cracked and leaks.

6. *Surely goodness and mercy shall follow me all the days of my life*. This is indisputable, and therefore a heavenly 'surely' is set as a seal upon it. This sentence may be read, 'Only goodness and mercy,' for there will be unmingled mercy in our story. These twin guardian angels will always be with me. Just as when great princes go abroad and must not go unattended, so it is with the believer. Goodness and mercy follow him always – the black days as well as the bright days. Goodness supplies our needs, and mercy blots out our sins.

And I will dwell in the house of the LORD for ever. A servant does not stay in the house for ever, but the son abides for ever. While I am here I will be a child at home with my God; the whole world will be his house to me; and when I ascend into the upper room I will not change my company, nor even change the house.

Psalm 121

1. *I will lift up mine eyes unto the hills, from whence cometh my help*. It is wise to look to the strong for strength. Dwellers in valleys are subject to many disorders for which there is no cure but a sojourn

in the uplands, and it is well when they shake off their lethargy and resolve upon a climb. Down below they are the prey of marauders, and to escape from them the surest method is to fly to the strongholds upon the mountains. Often before the actual ascent the sick and plundered people looked towards the hills and longed to be upon their summits. The holy man who here sings looked away from the slanderers by whom he was tormented to the Lord who saw all from the high places, and was ready to pour down succour for his injured servant. Help comes to saints only from above; they look elsewhere in vain. Let us lift up our eyes with hope, expectancy, desire, and confidence. Satan will endeavour to keep our eyes upon our sorrows that we may be disquieted and discouraged; be it ours firmly to resolve that we will look out and up, for there is good cheer for the eyes, and those who lift up their eyes to the eternal hills will soon have their hearts lifted up also. The purposes of God; the divine attributes; the immutable promises; the covenant, ordered in all things and sure; the providence, predestination, and proved faithfulness of the Lord – these are hills to which we must lift up our eyes, for from these our help must come. It is our resolve that we will not be bandaged and blindfolded, but will lift up our eyes.

Or is the text in the interrogative? Does he ask, 'Shall I lift up mine eyes to the hills?' Does he feel that the highest places of the earth can afford him no shelter? Or does he renounce the idea of recruits hastening to his standard from the hardy mountaineers? Does he again inquire, 'Whence cometh my help?'? If so, the next verse answers the question, and shows whence all help must come.

2. *My help cometh from the LORD, which made heaven and earth.* What we need is help – help powerful, efficient, constant: we need a very present help in trouble. What a mercy that we have it in our God. Our hope is in Jehovah, for our help comes from him. Help is on the road, and will not fail to reach us in due time, for he who sends it to us was never known to be too late. Jehovah who created all things is equal to every emergency; heaven and earth are at the disposal of him who made them, therefore let us be very joyful in

38

our infinite helper. He will sooner destroy heaven and earth than permit his people to be destroyed, and the perpetual hills themselves will bow rather than he fail whose ways are everlasting. We are bound to look beyond heaven and earth to him who made them both; it is vain to trust the creatures: it is wise to trust the Creator.

3. *He will not suffer thy foot to be moved*. Though the paths of life are dangerous and difficult, yet we shall stand fast, for Jehovah will not permit our feet to slide; and if he will not suffer it we shall not suffer it. If our feet will be thus kept we may be sure that our head and heart will be preserved also. In the original the words express a wish or prayer – 'May he not suffer thy foot to be moved'. Promised preservation should be the subject of perpetual prayer; and we may pray believingly, for those who have God for their keeper will be safe from all the perils of the way. Among the hills and ravines of Palestine the literal keeping of the feet is a great mercy; but in the slippery ways of a tried and afflicted life, the boon of upholding is of priceless value, for a single false step might cause us a fall fraught with awful danger. To stand erect and pursue the even tenor of our way is a blessing which only God can give, which is worthy of the divine hand, and worthy also of perennial gratitude. Our feet will move in progress, but they will not be moved to their overthrow.

He that keepeth thee will not slumber, or, 'thy keeper will not slumber'. We should not stand a moment if our keeper were to sleep; we need him by day and by night; not a single step can be safely taken except under his guardian eye. This is a choice stanza in a pilgrim song. God is the convoy and bodyguard of his saints. When dangers are awake around us we are safe, for our Preserver is awake also, and will not permit us to be taken unawares. No fatigue or exhaustion can cast our God into sleep; his watchful eyes are never closed.

4. *Behold, he that keepeth Israel shall neither slumber nor sleep*. The consoling truth must be repeated: it is too rich to be dismissed in a single line. It were well if we always imitated the sweet singer, and would dwell a little upon a choice doctrine, sucking the honey from it. What a glorious title is in the Hebrew – 'the Keeper of Israel' –

and how delightful to think that no form of unconsciousness ever steals over him, neither the deep slumber nor the lighter sleep. He will never let the house be broken up by the silent thief; he is ever on the watch, and speedily perceives every intruder. This is a subject of wonder, a theme for attentive consideration; therefore the word 'behold' is set up as a waymark. Israel fell asleep, but his God was awake. Jacob had neither walls, nor curtains, nor bodyguard around him; but the Lord was in that place though Jacob knew it not, and therefore the defenceless man was safe as in a castle. In after days he mentioned God under this enchanting name – 'The God that led me all my life long': perhaps David alludes to that passage in this expression. The word *keepeth* is also full of meaning: he keeps us as a rich man keeps his treasures, as a captain keeps a city with a garrison, as a royal guard keeps his monarch's head. If the previous verse is in strict accuracy a prayer, this is the answer to it. In verse 3 the Lord is spoken of as the personal keeper of one individual, and here of all those who are in his chosen nation, described as Israel: mercy to one saint is the pledge of blessing to them all. Happy are the pilgrims to whom this psalm is a safe-conduct; they may journey all the way to the celestial city without fear.

5. *The LORD is thy keeper*. Here the preserving One, who had been spoken of by pronouns in the two previous verses, is distinctly named – Jehovah. Here is a glorious person – 'Jehovah' – assuming a gracious office – 'keeper' – and fulfilling it in person on behalf of a favoured individual – 'thy' – and a firm assurance of revelation that it is so at this hour – 'is'. We may journey through the valley of the shadow of death and fear no evil.

The LORD is thy shade upon thy right hand. A shade gives protection from burning heat and glaring light. We cannot bear too much blessing; even divine goodness, which is a right-hand disposition, must be toned down and shaded to suit our infirmity, and this the Lord will do for us. God is as near us as our shadow, and we are as safe as angels.

6. *The sun shall not smite thee by day, nor the moon by night*. Doubtless there are dangers of the light and of the dark, but in both

40

and from both we shall be preserved – literally from excessive heat and from baneful chills; mystically from any injurious effects which might follow from doctrine; spiritually from the evils of prosperity and adversity; eternally from the strain of overpowering glory and from the pressure of terrible events, such as judgement. Day and night make up all time: thus the ever-present protection never ceases. All evil may be ranked as under the sun or the moon, and if neither of these can smite us we are indeed secure. God has not made a new sun or a fresh moon for his chosen; they exist under the same outward circumstances as others, but the power to smite is in their case removed from temporal agencies; saints are enriched, and not injured, by the powers which govern the earth's condition; to them has the Lord given 'the precious things brought forth by the sun, and the precious things brought forth by the moon', while at the same moment he has removed from them all bale and curse of heat or damp, of glare or chill.

7. *The LORD shall preserve thee from all evil.* It is a great pity that our admirable translation did not keep the word 'keep' all through the psalm, for all along it is one. God not only keeps his own in all evil times but from evil influences and operations, indeed from evils themselves. The wings of Jehovah amply guard his own from evils great and small, temporary and eternal. There is a most delightful double personality in this verse: Jehovah keep the believer, not by agents, but by himself; and the person protected is definitely pointed out by the word *thee* – it is not our estate or name which is shielded, but the proper person. To make this even more intensely real and personal another sentence is added: *The LORD shall preserve thee from all evil: he shall preserve thy soul*, or 'Jehovah will keep thy soul.' Soulkeeping is the soul of keeping. If the soul is kept. Our soul is kept from the dominion of sin, the infection of error, the crush of despondency, the puffing up of pride; kept from the world, the flesh, and the devil; kept for holier and greater things; kept in the love of God; kept unto the eternal kingdom and glory. What can harm a soul that is kept by the Lord?

8. *The LORD shall preserve thy going out and thy coming in from this time forth, and even for evermore.* When we go out in the morning to labour, and come home at eventide to rest, Jehovah will keep us. When we got out in youth to begin life, and come in at the end to die, we shall experience the same keeping. Our exits and our entrances are under one protection. Three times we have the phrase, 'Jehovah shall keep', as if the sacred Trinity thus sealed the word to make it sure: ought not all our fears to be slain by such a three-fold flight of arrows? This keeping is eternal, continuing from this time forth for evermore. The whole church is thus assured of everlasting security: the final perseverance of the saints is thus ensured, and the glorious immortality of believers is guaranteed. Under the aegis of such a promise we may go on pilgrimage without trembling, and venture into battle without dread. None are so safe as those whom God keeps, none so much in danger as the self-secure. To goings out and comings in belong particular dangers, since every change of position turns a fresh quarter to the foe, and it is for these weak points that an especial security is provided: Jehovah will keep the door when it opens and closes, and this he will perseveringly continue to do so long as there is left a single person who trusts in him, as long as a danger survives, and in fact as long as time endures. Glory be unto the Keeper of Israel, who is endeared to us under that title, since our growing sense of weakness makes us feel more deeply than ever our need of being kept.

Spurgeon's conversion

When I was in the hand of the Holy Spirit, under conviction of sin, I had a clear and sharp sense of the justice of God. Sin, whatever it might be to other people, became to me an intolerable burden. It was not so much that I feared hell, as that I feared sin; and all the while, I had upon my mind a deep concern for the honour of God's name, and the integrity of his moral government. I felt that it would not satisfy my conscience if I could be forgiven unjustly. But then there came the question – 'How could God be just, and yet justify me who had been so guilty?' I was worried and wearied with this question; neither could I see any answer to it. Certainly, I could never have invented an answer which would have satisfied my conscience. The doctrine of the atonement is to my mind one of the surest proofs of the divine inspiration of holy scripture. Who would or could have thought of the just ruler dying for the unjust rebel? This is no teaching of human mythology, or dream of poetical imagination. This method of expiation is only known among men because it is a fact; fiction could not have devised it. God himself ordained it; it is not a matter which could have been imagined. I had heard of the plan of salvation by the sacrifice of Jesus from my youth up; but I did not know any more about it in my innermost soul than if I had been born and bred a Hottentot. The light was there, but I was blind; it was of necessity that the Lord himself should make the matter plain to me. It came to me as a new revelation, as fresh as if I had never read in Scripture that Jesus was declared to be the propitiation for sins that God might be just. I believe it will have to come as a revelation to every new-born child of God whenever he sees it; I mean that glorious doctrine of the substitution of the Lord Jesus. I came to understand that salvation was possible through vicarious sacrifice. Inasmuch as our fall was not at the first a personal one, for we feel in our federal representative, the first Adam, it became possible for us to be recovered by a second representative, even by him who has undertaken to be the covenant head of his people, so as to be their second Adam.

When I was anxious about the possibility of a just God pardoning me, I understood and saw by faith that he who is the Son of God became man, and in his own blessed person bore my sin in his own body on the tree. I saw that the chastisement of my peace was laid on him, and that with his stripes I was healed. It was because the Son of God, supremely glorious in his matchless person, undertook to vindicate the law by bearing the sentence due to me, that therefore God was able to pass by my sin. My sole hope for heaven lies in the full atonement made upon Calvary's cross for the ungodly. Personally, I could never have overcome my own sinfulness. I tried and failed. My evil propensities were too many for me, till, in the belief that Christ died for me, I cast my guilty soul on him and then I received a conquering principle by which I overcame my sinful self. If Christ has died for me, ungodly as I am, without strength as I am, then I cannot live in sin any longer, but must arouse myself to love and serve him who has redeemed me. I cannot trifle with the evil which slew my best friend. I must be bold for his sake. How can I live in sin when he has died to save me from it?

There was a day, as I took my walks abroad, when I came hard by a spot for ever engraven upon my memory, for there I saw this friend, my best, my only friend, murdered. I stooped down in sad affright, and looked at him. I saw that his hands had been pierced with rough iron nails, and his feet had been rent in the same way.

44

There was misery in his dead countenance so terrible that I scarcely dared to look upon it. His body was emaciated with hunger, his back was red with bloody scourges, and his brow had a circle of wounds about it: clearly could one see that these had been pierced by thorns. I shuddered, for I had known this friend full well. He never had a fault; he was the purest of the pure, the holiest of the holy. We had never breathed out anything else but love; and as I looked into the poor sorrowful face, so full of agony, and yet so full of love, I wondered who could have been a wretch so vile as to pierce hands like his. I listened, and I clearly perceived that the murderer was close at hand. It was dark, and I groped about to find him. I found that somehow or other, wherever I put out my hand, I could not meet with him for he was nearer to me than my hand would go. At last I put my hand upon my breast, for he was in my own heart.

When my soul can, in imagination, see the Saviour bearing his cross to Calvary, she joins the godly women, and weeps with them; for, indeed, there is true cause for grief – cause lying deeper than those mourning women thought. Why those women loved and wept, it were not hard to guess; but they could not have had greater reasons for love and grief than my heart has. Nain's widow saw her son restored; but I myself have been raised to newness of life. Peter's wife's mother was cured of the fever; but I of the greater plague of sin. Out of Magdalene seven devils were cast; but a whole legion out of me. Mary and Martha were favoured with visits from him; but he dwells with me. His mother bare his body; but he is formed in me, 'the hope of glory'.

He knocked at the door of my heart, and I refused to open it. He came to me, times without number, morning by morning, and night by night; he checked me in my conscience, and spoke to me by his spirit, and when, at last, the thunders of the law prevailed in my conscience, I thought that Christ was cruel and unkind. But what a loving reception did I have when I went to him! I though he would smite me, but his hand was not clenched in anger, but opened wide in mercy. I thought full sure that his eyes would dart lightning-flashes of wrath upon me; but, instead of that, they were full of tears. He fell upon my neck, and kissed me; he took off my rags, and clothed me with his righteousness, and caused my soul to sing aloud for joy; while in the house of my heart, and in the house of his church, there was music and dancing, because his son that he had lost was found, and he that had been dead was made alive again.

In my conversion, the very point lay in making the discovery that I had nothing to do but to look to Christ, and I would be saved. I believe that I had been a very good, attentive hearer; my own impression about myself was that nobody ever listened much better than I did. For years, as a child, I tried to learn the way of salvation; and either I did not hear it set forth, which I think cannot quite have been the case, or else I was spiritually blind and deaf, and could not see it and could not hear it; but the good news that I was, as a sinner, to look away from myself to Christ, startled much as much, and came as fresh to me, as any news I ever heard in my life.

When, for the first time, I received the Gospel to my soul's salvation, I thought that I had never really heard it before, and I began to think that the preachers to whom I had listened had not truly preached it. But, on looking back, I am inclined to believe that I had heard the Gospel fully preached many hundreds of times before, and that this was the difference – that I then heard it as though I heard it not; and when I did hear it, the message may not have been any more clear in itself than it had been at former times, but the power of the Holy Spirit was present to open my ear, and to guide the message to my heart. When I first discovered what faith really was, and exercised it – for with me these two things came together, I believed as soon as ever I knew what believing meant – then I thought I had never before heard that truth preached. But, now, I am persuaded that the light often shone on my eyes, but I was blind, and therefore I thought that the light had never come there. The light was shining all the while, but there was no power to receive it.

I must always attach special value to the *hearing of the truth*, for by it I received the joy and peace in which my soul delights.

While under concern of soul, I resolved that I would attend all the places of worship in the town where I lived, in order that I might find out the way of salvation. I was willing to do anything, and be anything, if God would only forgive my sin. I set off, determined to go round to all the chapels, and I did go to every place of worship; but for a long time I went in vain. I do not, however, blame the ministers. One man preached divine sovereignty; I could hear him with pleasure, but what was that sublime truth to a poor sinner who wished to know what he must do to be saved? There was another admirable man who always preached about the law; but what was the use of ploughing up ground that needed to be sown? Another was a practical preacher. I heard him, but it was very much like a commanding officer teaching the manoeuvres of war to a set of men without feet. What could I do? All his exhortations were lost on me.

I knew it was said, 'Believe on the Lord Jesus Christ, and thou shalt be saved'; but I did not know what it was to believe on Christ. These good men all preached truths suited to many in their congregations who were spiritually minded people; but what I wanted to know was – 'How can I get my sins forgiven? – and they never told me that.

I sometimes think I might have been in darkness and despair until now had it not been for the goodness of God in sending a snowstorm, one Sunday morning, while I was going to a certain place of worship. When I could go no further, I turned down a side street, and came to a little Primitive Methodist Chapel. In that chapel there may have been a dozen or fifteen people. I had heard of the Primitive Methodists, how they sang so loudly that they made people's heads ache; but that did not matter to me. I wanted to know how I might be saved, and if they could tell me that, I did not care how much they made my head ache. The minister did not come that morning; he was snowed up, I suppose. At last, a very thin-looking man, a shoemaker, or tailor, or something of that sort, went up into the pulpit to preach. Now, it is well that preachers should be instructed; but this man was really stupid. He was obliged to stick to his text, for the simple reason that he had little else to say. The text was: 'Look unto me, and be ye saved, all the ends of the earth'. He did not even pronounce the words rightly, but that did not matter. There was, I thought, a glimpse of hope for me in that text. The preacher began thus:

My dear friends, this is a very simple text indeed. It says, 'Look'. Now lookin' don't take a deal of pains. It ain't liftin' your foot or your finger; it is just, 'Look'. Well, a man needn't go to college to learn to look. You may be the biggest fool, and yet you can look. A man needn't be worth a thousand a year to be able to look. Anyone can look; even a child can look. But then the text says, 'Look unto *me*'. Ay! [said he, in broad Essex] many on ye are lookin' to yourselves, but it's no use lookin' there. You'll never find any comfort in yourselves. Some look to God the Father. No, look to him by-and-by. Jesus Christ says, 'Look unto *me*'. Some on ye say, 'We must wait for the Spirit's workin'.' You have no business with that just now. Look to *Christ*. The text says, 'Look unto *me*'.

Then the good man followed up his text in this way:

Look unto me; I am sweating great drops of blood. Look unto me; I am hangin' on the cross. Look unto me; I am dead and buried. Look unto me; I am sittin' at the Father's right hand. O poor sinner, look unto me! Look unto me!

When he had gone to about that length, and managed to spin out ten minutes or so, he was at the end of his tether. Then he looked at me under the gallery, and I daresay, with so few present, he knew me to be a stranger. Just fixing his eyes on me, as if he knew all my heart, he said, 'Young man, you look very miserable'. Well, I did; but I had not been accustomed to have remarks made from the pulpit on my personal appearance before. However, it was a good blow, struck right home. He continued, 'and you always will be miserable – miserable in life, and miserable in death – if you don't obey my text; but if you obey now, this moment, you will be saved.'

Then, lifting up his hands, he shouted, as only a Primitive Methodist could do, 'Young man, look to Jesus Christ. Look! Look! Look! You have nothin' to do but to look and live.'

I saw at once the way of salvation. I know not what else he said – I did not take much notice of it – I was so possessed with that one thought. Just as when the brazen serpent was lifted up, the people only looked and were healed, so it was with me. I had been waiting to do fifty things, but when I heard that word, 'Look!' what a charming word it seemed to me! Oh! I looked until I could almost have looked my eyes away. There and then the cloud was gone, the darkness had rolled away, and that moment I saw the sun; and I could have risen that instant, and sung with the most enthusiastic of them of the precious blood of Christ, and the simple faith which looks alone to him.

That happy day, when I found the Saviour, and learned to cling to his dear feet, was a day never to be forgotten by me. An obscure child, unknown, unheard of, I listened to the Word of God; and that precious text led me to the cross of Christ. I can testify that the joy of that day was utterly indescribable. It is not everyone who can remember the very day and hour of his deliverance; but it was so with me. Between half-past ten o'clock, when I entered that chapel, and half-past twelve o'clock, when I was back again at home, what a change had taken place in me! I had passed from darkness into marvellous light, from death to life. Simply by looking to Jesus, I had been delivered from despair, and I was brought into such a joyous state of mind that, when they saw me at home, they said to me, 'Something wonderful has happened to you'; and I was eager to tell them all about it. Oh, there was joy in the household that day, when all heard that the eldest son had found the Saviour, and knew himself to be forgiven!

When I look back upon it, I can see one reason why the Word was blessed to me as I heard it preached in that Primitive Methodist Chapel at Colchester; I had been up early crying to God for the

49

blessing. As a lad, when I was seeking the Saviour, I used to rise with the sun, that I might get time to read gracious books, and to seek the Lord. I can recall the kind of pleas I used when I took my arguments, and came before the throne of grace: 'Lord, save me; it will glorify thy grace to save such a sinner as I am! Lord, save me, else I am lost to all eternity; do not let me perish, Lord! Save me, O Lord, for Jesus died! By his agony and bloody sweat, by his cross and passion, save me!'

I often proved that the early morning was the best part of the day; I liked those prayers of which the psalmist said, 'In the morning shall my prayer prevent thee'.

The Holy Spirit, who enabled me to believe, gave me peace through believing. I felt as sure that I was forgiven as before I felt sure of condemnation. I had been certain of my condemnation because the Word of God declared it, and my conscience bore witness to it; but when the Lord justified me, I was made equally certain by the same witnesses. The Word of the Lord in the Scripture says, 'He that believeth on him is not condemned', and my conscience bore witness that I believed, and that God in pardoning me was just. Thus I had the witness of the Holy Spirit and also of my own conscience, and these two agreed in one.

How can a man know that he is pardoned? There is a text which says, 'Believe on the Lord Jesus Christ, and thou shalt be saved'. I believe on the Lord Jesus Christ; is it irrational to believe that I am saved? 'He that believeth on the Son hath everlasting life;' says Christ, in John's Gospel. I believe on Christ; am I absurd in believing that I have eternal life? I find the apostle Paul speaking by the Holy Spirit, and saying, 'There is therefore now no condemnation to them that are in Christ Jesus. Being justified by faith, we have peace with God'. If I know that my trust is fixed on Jesus only, and that I have faith in him, were it not ten thousand times more absurd for me not to be at peace, than for me to be filled with joy unspeakable? It is but taking God at his Word, when the soul knows, as a necessary consequence of the faith, that it is saved.

I took Jesus as my Saviour, and I was saved; and I can tell the reason why I took him for my Saviour. To my own humiliation, I must confess that I did it because I could not help it; I was shut up to it. That stern law-work had hammered me into such a condition that, if there had been fifty other saviours, I could not have thought of them – I was driven to this one. I wanted a divine saviour, I wanted one who was made a curse for me, to expiate my guilt. I wanted one who had died, for I deserved to die. I wanted one who had risen again, who was able by his life to make me live. I wanted the exact Saviour that stood before me in the Word, revealed to my heart; and I could not help having him.

My evidence that I am saved does not lie in the fact that I preach, or that I do this or that. All my hope lies in this, that Jesus Christ came to save sinners. I am a sinner, I trust him, then he came to save me, and I am saved; I live habitually in the enjoyment of this blessed fact, and it is long since I have doubted the truth of it, for I have his own Word to sustain my faith. It is a very surprising thing, a thing to be marvelled at most of all by those who enjoy it. I know that it is to me even to this day the greatest wonder that I ever heard of, that God should ever justify me. I feel myself to be a lump of unworthiness, a mass of corruption, and a heap of sin, apart from his almighty love; yet I know by a full assurance that I am justified by faith which is in Christ Jesus, and treated as if I had been perfectly just, and made an heir of God and a joint-heir with Christ, though by nature I must take my place among the most sinful. I, who am altogether undeserving, am treated as if I had been deserving. I am loved with as much love as if I had always been godly, whereas before I was ungodly.

I have always considered, with Luther and Calvin, that the sum and substance of the Gospel less in that word *substitution* – Christ standing in the place of man. If I understand the Gospel, it is this: I deserve to be lost for ever; the only reason why I should not be damned is that Christ was punished in my place, and there is no need to execute a sentence twice for sin. On the other hand, I know I cannot enter heaven unless I have a perfect righteousness; I am absolutely certain I shall never have one of my own, for I find I sin every day; but then Christ had a perfect righteousness, and he said, 'There, poor sinner, take my garment, and put it on; you shall stand before God as if you were Christ, and I will stand before God as if I had been a sinner; I will suffer in the sinner's place, and you shall be rewarded for works which you did not do, but which I did for you'. I find it very convenient every day to come to Christ as a sinner, as I came at the first. 'You are no saint,' says the devil. Well, if I am not, I am a sinner, and Jesus Christ came into the world to save sinners.

Finally, I bear my witness that he is full of truth. His promises have been true; not one has failed. I have often doubted him; for that I blush. He has never failed me; in this I must rejoice. I bear witness that never servant had such a master as I have; never brother had such a kinsman as he has been to me; never spouse had such a husband as Christ has been to my soul; never sinner a better saviour; never soldier a better captain; never mourner a better comforter than Christ has been to my spirit. I want none beside him. In life, he is my life; and in death, he will be the death of death; in poverty, Christ is my riches; in sickness, he makes my bed; in darkness, he is my star; and in brightness, he is my sun. By faith I understand that the blessed son of God redeemed my soul with his own heart's blood; and by sweet experience I know that he raised me up from the pit of dark despair, and set my feet on the rock. He died for me. This is the root of every satisfaction I have. He put all my transgressions away. He cleansed me with his precious blood; he covered me with his perfect righteousness; he wrapped me up in his own virtues. He has promised to keep me, while I abide in this world, from its temptations and snares; and when I depart from this world, he has already prepared for me a mansion in the heaven of unfading bliss, and a crown of everlasting joy that will never, never fade away.

What more can I wish than that, while my brief term on earth lasts, I should be the servant of him who became the servant of servants for me? I can say, concerning Christ's religion, if I had to die like a dog, and had no hope whatever of immortality, if I wanted to lead a happy life, let me serve my God with all my heart; let me be a follower of Jesus, and walk in his footsteps. If there were no here-after, I would still prefer to be a Christian, and the humblest Christian minister, to being a king or an emperor, for I am persuaded there are more delights in Christ, indeed more joy in one glimpse of his face, than is to be found in all the praises of this harlot world, and in all the delights which it can yield to us in its sunniest and brightest days.

I have seen hundreds and thousands who have given their hearts to Jesus, but I never did see one who said he was disappointed with him; I never met with one who said Jesu Christ was less than he was declared to be. When first my eyes beheld him, when the burden slipped from off my heavy-laden shoulders, and I was free from condemnation, I thought that all the preachers I had ever heard had not half preached, they had not told half the beauty of my Lord and master. So good! So generous! So gracious! So willing to forgive! It seemed to me as if they had almost slandered him; they painted his likeness, doubtless, as well as they could, but it was a mere smudge compared with the matchless beauties of his face. All who have ever seen him want the same always. I go back to my home, many a time, mourning that I cannot preach my Master even as I myself know him, and what I know of him is very little compared with the matchlessness of his grace. Would that I knew more of him, and that I could tell it out better.

'I believe in conversion'

There are some passages of Scripture which have been more abundantly blessed to the conversion of souls than others have; they may be called salvation texts. We may not be able to discover how it is, or why it is; but certainly it is the fact that some chosen verses have been more used of God than any others in his Word to bring men to the cross of Christ. They are not more inspired than other parts of the Bible; but I suppose they are more noticeable, from their position, or from their peculiar phraseology they are more adapted to catch the eye of the reader, and are more suitable to a widely prevailing spiritual condition. All the stars in the heavens shine very brightly. One of the chief of those texts is Isaiah 43:25: 'I, even I, am he that blotteth out thy transgressions for mine own sake, and will not remember thy sins.'

Some who come to see me with the view of joining the church cannot say much, and they think that I shall be very dissatisfied with them because they make a great muddle of their narrative; but the people with whom I am least satisfied are those who reel off their yarn by the yard; they have it all ready to repeat, and everything is arranged as prettily as possible. As I listen to it, I know that someone has told them what to say, and they have learned it all for me to hear. I like far better the testimony that I have to pick out in little bits, but which I know comes fresh from the heart of the trembling convert.

Christ's lovely character

Among the many thousands of souls who have been brought to know the Lord under my instrumentality, I have often noticed that a considerable portion of these, and of the best members of our church, too, were won to the Saviour not by legal terrors, but by gentler means. I asked an excellent young woman, 'What was the first thought that set you really seeking the Saviour?'

'Oh, sir!' she replied, 'it was Christ's lovely character that first made me long to be his disciple. I saw how kind, how good, how disinterested, how self-sacrificing he was, and that made me feel how different I was. I thought, "Oh! I am not like Jesus!" and that sent me to my room, and I began to pray, and so I came to trust in him.'

Fear of future sin

'The first religious impression I ever had,' said another, 'that set me seeking the Saviour, was this: a young companion of mine fell into sin, and I knew that I was likely to do the same if I was not kept by someone stronger than myself. I therefore sought the Lord, not so much at first on account of past transgression, but because I was afraid of some great future sin. God visited me, and I then felt conviction of sin, and was brought to Christ.'

It is not true that all who are saved suffer the same such convictions and terrors as some of us had to endure; there are very many who are drawn with the cords of a man and the bands of love. There are some who, like Lydia, have their hearts opened, not by the crowbar of conviction, but by the picklock of divine grace.

Saved there and then

A young woman came to me one day after a service to ask me whether I really meant what I said when I declared that he that believed in Jesus Christ was saved there and then. 'Yes,' I replied; and I gave her the scriptural warrant for the statement.

'Why!' she exclaimed, 'my grandfather told me that, when he found religion, it took him six months, and they nearly had to put

55

him in a lunatic asylum, he was in such a dreadful state of mind.'

'Well,' I answered, 'that sometimes happens; but that distress of his did not save him. That was simply his conscience and Satan together keeping him away from Christ. When he was saved, it was not by his deep feelings; it was by his believing in Jesus Christ.' I then went on to set the Saviour before her as our sole ground of hope in opposition to inward feelings.

'I see it,' she said; and I rejoiced as I noticed the bright light that passed over her face, a flash of heavenly sunshine which I have often seen on the countenances of those who have believed in Jesus Christ, when peace fills the soul even to the brim, and lights up the countenance with a minor transfiguration. Scores of times, when I have been talking with those who have been utterly bowed down beneath sin's burden, they have looked as though they were qualifying for an asylum through inward grief; but as soon as they have caught this thought, 'Christ stood as the Substitute for me; and if I trust in him, I have the proof that he did so, and I am clear,' their faces have been lit up as with the very glory of heaven.

Misled by others

Some people have come to me for spiritual guidance because they have been misled by others. One lady who called upon me said that she had not heard me preach, but she had been reading my sermons, and God had been pleased to bless them to her, not only to her conviction, but to her conversion. She went to the clergyman of the parish, full of joy at having found the Saviour, and began to tell him of her gladness, and how she rejoiced that all her sins were blotted out. He stopped her, and said, 'My good woman, that is all a delusion; you have no right to believe that your sins are pardoned, till you have led several years of piety and devotion.' She went away sad, and she came to ask me if what the clergyman said was true; and when I quoted that verse –

The moment a sinner believes,
  And trusts in his crucified God,
His pardon at once he receives,
  Redemption in full through his blood.

'Oh!', she said, 'I see it clearly now!' And when I went on to tell her that many who had believed in Christ had been black sinners one moment and white as snow the next, by casting themselves simply on Christ, they had instantly found peace, she could not but take to her heart the precious promises of Christ, and, believing in Jesus, being justified by faith, she had the peace of God that passes all understanding, and she went away rejoicing in Jesus.

'I do not know how to repent enough'

I received a letter from a young man who wrote: 'I have heard it said that we must all think ourselves to be the wickedest people in the world, or else we cannot be saved. I try to think so, but I cannot, because I have not been the wickedest. I want to be saved, but I do not know how to repent enough.'

Of course, I told him that God does not require every man to think himself the wickedest in the world, because that would sometimes be to think a falsehood, for there are some men who are not so sinful as others are. What God requires is that a man should say, 'I know more of myself than I do of other people; and from what I see of myself, not merely of my actions, but of my heart, I do think there can be few worse than I am. They may be more wicked openly, but then I have had more light, more privileges, more opportunities, more warnings, and therefore I am, in my own opinion at least, more guilty than they are.'

'I could not feel my need of Christ'

An excellent and amiable young woman, when converted to God, said to me: 'You know, sir, I used almost to wish that I was one of those very bad sinners whom you so often invited to come to Jesus, because I thought then I should feel my need more; that was my

57

difficulty. I could not feel my need of Christ.' It is a pity that any should make a hindrance of this matter; yet they do, and others make a difficulty for the opposite reason: they say, 'Oh, we could trust Christ if we had been kept from sin.' The fact is that unbelieving souls will not trust Christ whichever way they have lived; for, from some quarter or other, they will find cause for doubting; but, when the Lord the Spirit gives them faith, big sinners will trust Christ quite as readily as those who have not been great offenders openly; and those who have been preserved from open sin will trust him as joyfully as the vilest transgressors.

A sailor called 'Satan'

There was a man known in the village where he lived by the name of Satan, because of his being so thoroughly depraved. He was a sailor, and as another seaman in that place had been the means of conversion of all the sailors in a vessel belonging to the port, this man desired to sail with him to try and beat his religion out of him. He did his best – or rather, his worst – but he signally failed; and when the ship came to London, the Christian man asked the ungodly one whether he would come to the Tabernacle. He did not mind coming to hear me, for, as it happened, I was brought up near the place where he lived. This 'Satan' came on the Lord's Day morning when the text was upon soul-murder; and, by the Holy spirit's gracious application of the Word to his heart, he sat and sobbed, and cried under the sermon at such a rate that he could only say, 'People are noticing me; I had better go out'. But his companion would not let him go out; and from that day forth he became a new creature in Christ Jesus.

A poor outcast of society

On another occasion, on a Lord's Day meeting, I preached upon the word of the leper who said to Jesus, 'Lord, if thou wilt, thou canst make me clean'. On the following Thursday morning I received this letter: 'Dear Sir, I feel so happy to tell you that the Lord has pardoned a poor outcast of society. I got into your place in a crowd, hoping nobody would see me. I had been out all night, and was miserable. While you were preaching about the leper, my whole life of sin rose up before me. I saw myself worse than the leper, cast away by everybody; there is not a sin I was not guilty of. As you went on, I looked straightaway to Jesus. A gracious answer came: "Thy sins, which are many, are forgiven." I never heard any more of your sermon, I felt such joy to think that Jesus died even for a poor harlot. Long before you get this letter, I trust to be on the way to my dear home I ran away from . . .'

If it had not been for that sentence about going home, I might have had some doubt concerning her conversion; but when a fallen girl goes home to her father and mother, it is a sure case.

A religious man
One brother, when he was giving his testimony before being baptized, said: 'The first time I came to hear Mr Spurgeon in the Tabernacle, if you had asked me about myself, I should have told you that I was as religious a man as ever lived in Newington, and as good a man, certainly, as ever formed part of any congregation; but all this was reversed when I heard the Gospel that day. I came out of the building with every feather plucked out of me. I felt myself the most wretched sinner who could be on the face of the earth, and I said, "I will never go to hear that man again, for he has altogether spoiled me." But that was the best thing which could have happened to me. I was made to look away from myself, and all that I could do, to God, and to his omnipotent grace, and to understand that I must pass under my Creator's hand again, or I could never see his face with joy. I learned to loathe my own righteousness as filthy rags, fit only for the fire, and then I sought to be robed in the perfect righteousness of Christ.'

A Jew points the way
Another man who came to join with us in church-fellowship owed his conversion, indirectly, to a Jew. He was on a bus going by the Tabernacle, one Sunday, and a crowd was standing outside, as

usual, waiting for the doors to be opened. The person sitting next to him was a well-known Jew.

'Ah!' said the man, 'That humbug always attracts people.'

The Jew turned round to him and inquired, 'Would you not like to see such a crowd as that round your shop? I should welcome them at my place of business. I have ridden past here these twenty-eight years, and have always seen just such a crowd as that waiting to get in. Now, if your shop had been crowded thus for twenty-eight years, and anybody said that you did not sell a good article, what would you reply? You would probably answer that those people were good judges, and that, if you have not supplied goods that were satisfactory, they would not have kept on coming. Now I am a Jew, yet I am inclined to go in and listen to what Mr Spurgeon has to say, because I see these crowds of people going to hear him.'

The man who had at first made the offensive remark was greatly impressed by his companion's observation, and in telling us how it affected him, he said, 'I discovered that I had been buying the wrong article, and I thought the Jew had spoken very sensibly, so I resolved to go, and see and hear for myself.' He came, examined the article that was offered for sale, and bought it on the Gospel terms, 'without money and without price'.

Talking with a daughter

One Sabbath evening, while preaching in the Tabernacle, I felt moved to say: 'Dear mother, if you have never talked with your daughter about her soul, do it this very night. "But", you reply, "When I get home, she will be in bed." If so, than wake her up, but do talk and pray with her tonight; and then let her fall asleep again; begin at once this holy service if you have neglected it until now.'

One good woman who was present went straight home, and did exactly what I had said; she woke her daughter up, and began speaking to her about the Saviour. The dear girl said, 'Oh, mother, I am glad you have spoken to me about Jesus; for months I have been wishing you would do so.' It was not long before the mother brought her daughter to see me about joining the church, and then told me how the blessing had come to her.

Pencil and paper

On various occasions the Lord has set his seal upon a very simple request that I made to my congregation. I asked those who were present, after they reached their homes, to spend a little time quietly and alone, and then, when they had honestly considered their condition in the sight of God, to take a pencil and paper, and to write one of two words. If they felt that they were not believers in the Lord Jesus Christ, I asked them to write the word *Condemned*; but if they were trusting Jesus Christ, I asked them to put on the paper the word *Forgiven*. Several friends were brought to decision for Christ in that way; amongst them was one young man who, at first, wrote the word *Condemned*, but, as he looked at it, his tears began to flow, and his heart began to break; and before long he fled to Christ, put the paper in the fire, took another piece, wrote on it the word *Forgiven*, and soon came to tell me the good news, and to ask that he might be admitted to church-fellowship.

In another case, a man went home, and told his wife that he was going to write the word *Condemned*. She pleaded with him in vain, for he took the pencil, and was just about to make the letter C, but his little daughter, a Christian girl, caught hold of his hand and said, 'No, father, you shall not write it.' And by the united entreaties of his wife and child, the man was brought to the Saviour, and afterwards became a member with them at the Tabernacle.

Mysterious ways

My experience goes to show that there have been people converted to God by doctrines that some might have thought altogether unlikely to produce that result. I have known the doctrine of the resurrection to bring sinners to Christ; I have heard of scores brought to the Saviour by a discourse upon election – the very sort of people who, as far as I can see, would never have been reached if that truth had not happened to be an angular doctrine that just struck their heart in the right place, and fitted into the crevices of their nature. I have often preached a terrible sermon upon the law, and afterwards found that sinners had been comforted by it. God frequently blesses the Word in the very opposite manner to that in which I thought it would be blessed, and he brings very, very many to know their state by nature by doctrines which I should have thought would rather have comforted believers than awakened the unconverted. I am constantly driven back to the great foundation truth of divine sovereignty, and am made to realize that, in grace as well as in providence, 'God moves in a mysterious way, His wonders to perform'.

A runaway son

I was talking one day with an aged minister; and I noticed that he put his hand into his waistcoat pocket and brought out a letter that was well-nigh worn to pieces. As he unfolded it, he exclaimed, 'God Almighty bless you, sir! God Almighty bless you, sir!' I said, 'Thank you, my dear sir, for that blessing, but what makes you give it to me?' The good man replied, 'I had a son who I thought would be the stay of my old age, but he disgraced himself and ran away from home, and I could not tell where he had gone, only that he said he was going to America.' When the minister had told me so much of his story, he bade me read the letter, which ran thus:

Dear Father,
I am here in America; I have found a situation, and God has prospered me. I write to ask your forgiveness for the many wrongs that I have done you, and the grief I have caused you; and to tell you that, blessed be God, I have found the Saviour. I have joined the church here, and hope to spend my life in the Redeemer's service. This great change happened thus. I did not sail for America on the day I expected to start; and, having a leisure hour, I went down to the Tabernacle to see what it was like, and there God met with me. In his sermon, Mr

Spurgeon said, 'Perhaps there is a runaway son here. The Lord call him by his grace!' And he did call me.

'Now,' said the minister as he folded up the letter and put it into his pocket again, 'this son of mine is dead, and he has gone to heaven; and I love you, and shall continue to do so as long as I live, because you were the means of bringing him to Christ.'

Two inquirers

Two enquiring ones came to me in my vestry. They had been hearing the Gospel from me for only a short time, but they had been deeply impressed by it. They expressed their regret that they were about to move far away, but they added their gratitude that they had heard me at all. I was cheered by their kind thanks, but felt anxious that a more effectual work should be wrought in them, and therefore I asked them, 'Have you in very deed believed in the Lord Jesus Christ? Are you saved?'

One of them replied, 'I have been trying hard to believe.' I have often heard this statement, but I will never let it go by unchallenged.

'No,' I said, 'that will not do. Did you ever tell your father that you tried to believe him?'

After I had dwelt awhile upon the matter, they admitted that such language would have been an insult to their father. I then set the Gospel very plainly before them in a simple language as I could, and I begged them to believe Jesus, who is more worthy of faith than the best of fathers.

One of them replied, 'I cannot realize it; I cannot realize that I am saved.'

Then I went on to say, 'God bears testimony to his Son that whosoever trusts in the Lord Jesus Christ is saved. Will you make him a liar now, or will you believe his Word?'

While I was saying this, one of them started as if astonished, and she startled us all as she cried, 'Oh sir, I see it all; I am saved! Do bless Jesus for me; he has shown me the way, and he has saved me. I see it all.' The esteemed sister who had brought these friends to me knelt down with them while with all our hearts we blessed and magnified the Lord for a soul brought into the light. The other young woman, however, could not see the Gospel as her companion had done, though I feel sure she will do so; but it seemed strange that, both hearing the same words, one should come out into clear light, and the other should remain in the gloom.

Resisting the truth

When talking with anxious inquirers, I am often amazed at the ingenuity with which they resist the entrance of the truth into their hearts. I do not think I have ever been so much astonished at the invention of locomotive engines, electric telegraphs, or any other feats of human mechanism, as I have been at the marvellous aptitude of simple people in finding out reasons why they should not believe in the Lord Jesus Christ. After I have proved to them to a demonstration that it is the most reasonable and fitting thing in the world for them to trust themselves with Christ, they ask, 'How is this to be done?' and they argue, first one way, and then another, all against their own best interests. Often, I go patiently through the whole process again and again; and even when that has been done, there comes another objection. I have tracked these people to their holes as diligently as if I had been a fox-hunter, and I have tried to unearth them from their hiding-places; but I find that they can often burrow faster than I can follow them. Oh, the 'ifs' and 'buts' they put; the 'perhaps' and 'don't feel this' and 'I don't feel that'! Oh, that wicked questioning of Christ! While talking with them, endeavouring to comfort them, and I hope not unsuccessfully, I am often led to realize more deeply than before, in my own mind, what an awful crime it is to doubt God, to doubt him who speaks from above, to doubt him who hung bleeding on the tree.

Sitting, one day, to see inquirers, a young Dutchman came into the room. He had crossed from Flushing, and desired to tell me his difficulties of soul. He began, 'Sir, I cannot trust Christ'.

My answer was, 'Why not? What has he done that you should speak so ill of him? I have trusted everything in his hands, and I believe him to be quite trustworthy. What do you know against his character?'

'Indeed, sir, I know nothing against him, and I am ashamed that I have so spoken, for I believe the Lord Jesus to be worthy of all confidence. That was not what I meant. May I trust him to save me?'

'Of course you may, for you are commanded to do so by the Gospel, which says, "Believe on the Lord Jesus Christ, and thou shalt be saved." You are warned against not believing by the words, "He that believeth not shall be damned." '

'I may, then, trust Christ; but does he promise to save all who trust in him?'

'Certainly. I have already quoted to you the promise of the Gospel. It is also written, "Whosoever shall call upon the name of the Lord shall be saved." If Jesus does not save you upon your trusting him, you will be the first he ever cast out.'

'Ah, sir, I see it! Why did I not see it before? I trust, and Jesus saves me. I am well repaid for coming from Flushing.'

I prayed with him, and he went his way trembling for joy.

'Will you pray for me?'
A lady came to me after a service in the Tabernacle, and asked me to pray for her. She had been before to speak to me about her soul, so I said to her, on the second occasion, 'I told you very plainly the way of salvation, namely, that you are to trust yourself in Christ's hands, relying on his atoning sacrifice. Have you done that?'

She answered, 'No,' and then asked me whether I would pray for her.

I said, 'No, certainly I will not.'

She looked at me with astonishment, and again asked, 'Will you not pray for me?'

'No,' I replied, 'I have nothing for which to pray for you. I have set the way of salvation before you so simply that, if you will not walk in it, you will be lost; but if you trust Christ now, you will be saved. I have nothing further to say to you; but, in God's name, to set before you life or death.'

Still she pleaded, 'Do pray for me!'

'No,' I answered. 'Would you have me ask God to shape his Gospel so as to let you in as an exception? I do not see why he should. His plan of salvation is the only one that ever has been or ever will be of any avail; and if you will not trust to it, I am not going to ask God anything, for I do not see what else is wanted from him. I put this question plainly to you: "Will you believe in the Lord Jesus Christ?" '

I certainly was somewhat surprised when the sister said, very deliberately, 'If it be so, then, that salvation will come to me by believing, I do believe what the Scripture says concerning Christ; and, moreover, I feel that I can trust myself with him, because he is God, and he has offered a sufficient sacrifice for my sins; and I do trust myself to him just now; and I feel such a strange peace stealing over me at this very moment. I have trusted him, and I am certain that I am saved.' And in an instant she said to me, 'Good evening, sir; there are other people waiting to see you,' and away she went, like a common-sense woman as she was; and she has often told me, since, how glad she was that I refused to pray for her, and so brought her to the decision to trust Christ for herself, and thus to receive the assurance of her salvation.

A feeble start

There is a great contrast between the way in which different converts begin their new life. I have sometimes thought that, if a man does not become a high-class Christian during the first three months after his conversion, he probably never will. I have noticed some people who have commenced their Christian career in a very feeble fashion. I hope they so began that they were really saved; but, still, they started doubting and fearing, and they kept on in the same style till they went to heaven.

'Ah, sir!' said one to me once, 'Either all the world has altered, or else I have, for people I once delighted in I am now afraid of. The things that once made me glad now make me unhappy, and those that I thought melancholy are now the very things in which I find my highest joy.'

I am always thankful when our friends get a very decided conversion, because, though I am not going to say a word against those who come to Christ very gradually, yet their experience is rather cloudy. No doubt they are just as safe as others, but they lack a good deal of comfort afterwards; and sometimes people who are very readily converted, and who have no very deep sense of sin, are more apt to play with evil than others are who have had a clearer sight of its enormity. Some begin by serving the Lord stingily, not giving him their whole hearts; or they commence coldly, and so they never get hot with zeal all their lives. I am glad when a young convert is red-hot, or even white-hot; I like to see him too full of zeal, if that is possible; because, when he cools down, he will come just to the right temperature if he is too hot at first; but, if he is cool at the beginning, what will he come to by and by? There are no labourers for the Master who are so useful as those who begin to serve him while they are young. Sometimes, God converts men in middle life, or even in old age, and uses them in his service; but, still, I venture to assert that church history will show that the most useful servants of Christ were those who were caught early, and who from their youth up bore testimony to the Gospel of Jesus. In the case of some old people, who have professed religion for years but have done next to nothing for Christ, I find it very difficult ever to stir them up at all. When I do get a saddle on them, they are very restive creatures, like a horse that has never been broken in; but if I break them in while they are colts, they get used to their work, it becomes a delight to them, and they would not be happy unless they had something to do for the Lord Jesus. I remember having a considerable share of sneers, and not a few rebukes, from some who thought themselves very wise men, because I began preaching at the age of sixteen. I was recommended to tarry at Jericho till my beard had grown, and a great many other pieces of advice were

given to me; but I have never regretted that I was a 'boy-preacher';
and if I could have my time over again, I would like to do just the
same as I did then.

The Cheque Book
of the Bank of Faith

'And there shall ye remember your ways, and all your doings, wherein ye have been defiled; and ye shall loathe yourselves in your own sight for all your evils that ye have committed' (Ezekiel 20:43).

When we are accepted by the Lord, and are standing in the place of favour, and peace, and safety, then we are led to repent of all our failures and miscarriages towards our gracious God. So precious is repentance that we may call it a diamond of the first water, and this is sweetly promised to the people of God as one most sanctifying result of salvation. He who accepts repentance also gives repentance; and he gives is not out of 'the bitter box', but from among those 'wafers made with honey' on which he feeds his people. A sense of blood-bought pardon and of undeserved mercy is the best means of dissolving a heart of stone. Are we feeling hard? Let us come to God with this promise of penitence, and ask him to help us to remember, and repent, and regret, and return. Oh that we could enjoy the meltings of holy sorrow! What a relief would a flood of tears be! Lord, smite the rock, or speak to the rock, and cause the waters to flow!

> '*When a man's ways please the Lord, he maketh even his enemies to be at peace with him*' (Proverbs 16:7).

I must see that my ways please the Lord. Even then I shall have enemies; and perhaps all the more certainly because I endeavour to do that which is right. But what a promise is this! The Lord will make the wrath of man to praise him, and abate it so that it will not distress me.

He can constrain an enemy to desist from harming me, even though he has a mind to do so. This he did with Laban, who pursued Jacob, but did not dare to touch him. Or he can subdue the wrath of the enemy, and make him friendly, as he did with Esau, who met Jacob in a brotherly manner, though Jacob had dreaded that he would smite him and his family with the sword. The Lord can also convert a furious adversary into a brother in Christ, and a fellow-worker, as he did with Saul of Tarsus. Oh that he would do this in every case where a persecuting spirit appears!

Happy is the man whose enemies are made to be to him what the lions were to Daniel in the den: quiet and companionable! When I meet death, who is called the last enemy, I pray that I may be at peace. Only let my great care be to please the Lord in all things. Oh for faith and holiness; for these are a pleasure unto the Most High!

> '*They shall be mine, saith the Lord of hosts, in that day when I make up my jewels*' (Malachi 3:17).

A day is coming in which the crown jewels of our great King will be counted to see if they match the inventory which his Father gave him. My soul, will you be among the precious things of Jesus? You are precious to him if he is precious to you, and you will be his 'in that day', if he is precious to you today.

In the days of Malachi, those chosen by the Lord were accustomed so to converse with each other that their God himself listened to their talk. He liked it so much that he took notes of it; yes, and made a book of it, which he lodged in his Record Office.

70

Pleased with their conversation, he was also pleased with them. Pause, my soul, and ask yourself: If Jesus were to listen to your talk would he be pleased with it? Is it to his glory and to the edification of the brotherhood? Say, my soul, and be sure you say the truth.

But what will the honour be for us poor creatures to be reckoned by the Lord to be his crown jewels! All the saints have this honour. Jesus not only says, 'They are mine,' but, 'They will be mine.' He bought us, sought us, brought us in, and has so far wrought us to his image that we shall be fought for by him with all his might.

'*And the priest shall put some of the blood upon the horns of the altar of sweet incense before the Lord*' (Leviticus 4:7).

The altar of incense is where saints present their prayers and praises; and it is delightful to think of it as sprinkled with the blood of the great sacrifice. It is this which makes all our worship acceptable to Jehovah: he sees the blood of his own Son, and therefore accepts our homage.

It is well for us to fix our eyes upon the blood of the one offering for sin. Sin mingles even with our holy things, and our best repentance, faith, prayer, and thanksgiving could not be received by God were it not for the merit of the atoning sacrifice. Many sneer at 'the blood'; but to us it is the foundation of comfort and hope. That which is on the horns of the altar is meant to be prominently before our eyes when we draw near to God. The blood gives strength to prayer, and hence it is on the altar's horns. It is 'before the Lord', and therefore it ought to be before us. It is on the altar before we bring the incense; it is there to sanctify our offerings and gifts.

Come, let us pray with confidence, since the victim is offered, the merit has been pleaded, the blood is within the veil, and the prayers of believers must be sweet unto the Lord.

'*And it shall be forgiven them; for it is ignorance*'
(Numbers 15:25).

Because of our ignorance we are not fully aware of our sins of ignorance. Yet we may be sure they are many, in the form both of commission and omission. We may be doing in all sincerity, as a service to God, that which he has never commanded, and can never accept.

The Lord knows these sins of ignorance every one. This may well alarm us, since in justice he will require these trespasses at our hand; but on the other hand, faith spies comfort in this fact, for the Lord will see to it that stains unseen by us shall yet be washed away. He sees the sin that he may cease to see it by casting it behind his back.

Our great comfort is that Jesus, the true priest, has made atonement for all the congregation of the children of Israel. That atonement secures the pardon of unknown sins. His precious blood cleanses us from all sin. Whether or not our eyes have seen it and wept over it, God has seen it, Christ has atoned for it, the Spirit bears witness to the pardon of it, and so we have a threefold peace.

O my Father, I praise your divine knowledge, which not only perceives my iniquities, but provides an atonement which delivers me from the guilt of them, even before I know that I am guilty.

'*I shall not die, but live, and declare the works of the Lord*' (Psalm 118:17).

A fair assurance this! It was no doubt based upon a promise, inwardly whispered in the psalmist's heart, which he seized upon and enjoyed. Is my case like that of David? Am I depressed because the enemy insults over me? Are there multitudes against me, and few on my side? Does unbelief bid me lie down and die in despair – a defeated, dishonoured man? Do my enemies begin to dig my grave?

What then? Shall I yield to the whisper of fear, and give up the battle, and with it give up all hope? Far from it. There is life in me yet: 'I shall not die.' Vigour will return and remove my weakness: 'I shall live.' The Lord lives, and I shall live also. My mouth will again be opened: 'I shall declare the works of Jehovah.' Yes, and I will speak of the present trouble as another instance of the wonder-working faithfulness and love of the Lord my God. Those who would gladly measure me for my coffin had better wait a bit; for 'the Lord hath chastened me sore, but he hath not given me over unto death'. Glory be to his name for ever! I am immortal until my work is done. Till the Lord will sit no vault can close upon me.

'*No good thing will he withhold from them that walk uprightly*' (Psalm 84:11).

Many pleasing things the Lord may withhold, but 'no good thing'. He is the best judge of what is good for us. Some things are assuredly good, and these we may have for the asking through Jesus Christ our Lord.

Holiness is a good thing, and this he will work in us freely. Victory over evil tendencies, strong tempers, and evil habits, he will gladly grant, and we ought not to remain without it.

Full assurance he will bestow, and *close communion* with himself, and *access* into all truth, and *boldness* with prevalence at the mercy seat. If we do not have these, it is from lack of faith to receive, and not from any unwillingness of God to give. A calm, a heavenly frame, *great patience*, and *fervent love* – all these he will give to holy diligence.

But note well that we must 'walk uprightly'. There must be no cross purposes and crooked dealings; no hypocrisy or deceit. If we walk foully God cannot give us favours, for that would be a premium upon sin. The way of uprightness is the way of heavenly wealth – wealth so large as to include every good thing.

What a promise to plead in prayer! Let us get to our knees.

'*If ye shall ask anything in my name, I will do it*' (John 14:14).

What a wide promise! Anything! Whether large or small, all my needs are covered by that word 'anything'. Come, my soul, be free at the mercy seat, and hear your Lord saying to you, 'Open thy mouth wide, and I will fill it'.

What a wise promise! We are always to ask in the name of Jesus. While this encourages *us*, it also honours *him*. This is a constant plea. Occasionally every other plea is darkened, especially such as we could draw from our own relation to God, or our experience of his grace; but at such times the name of Jesus is as mighty at the throne as ever, and we may plead it with full assurance.

What an instructive prayer! I may not ask for anything to which I dare not put Christ's hand and seal. I dare not use my Lord's name to a selfish or wilful petition. I may only use my Lord's name to prayers which he would himself pray if he were in my case. It is a high privilege to be authorized to ask in the name of Jesus as if Jesus himself asked; but our love to him will never allow us to set that name where he would not have set it.

Am I asking for that which Jesus approves? Dare I put his seal to my prayer? Then I have that which I seek of the Father.

'*And he said, My presence shall go with thee, and I will give thee rest*' (Exodus 33:14).

Precious promise! Lord, enable me to appropriate it as all my own.

We must go at certain times from our abode, for here we have no continuing city. It often happens that when we feel most at home in a place, we are suddenly called away from it. Here is the antidote for this ill. The Lord himself will keep us company. His presence, which includes his favour, his fellowship, his care, and his power, will always be with us in every one of our marchings. This means far more than it says; for, in fact, it means all things. If we have God present with us, we have possession of heaven and earth. Go with me, Lord, and then command me wherever you will!

But we hope to find a place of rest. The text promises it. We are to have rest of God's own giving, making, and preserving. His presence will cause us to rest even when we are on the march, indeed, even in the midst of battle. *Rest*! Thrice blessed word. Can it ever be enjoyed by mortals? Yes, there is the promise, and by faith we plead it. Rest comes from the Comforter, from the Prince of Peace, and from the glorious Father who rested on the seventh day from all his works. To be with God is to rest in the most emphatic sense.

'*The Lord will give strength unto his people; the Lord will bless his people with peace*' (Psalm 29:11).

David had just heard the voice of the Lord in a thunderstorm, and had seen his power in the hurricane whose path he had described; and now, in the cool calm after the storm, that overwhelming power by which heaven and earth are shaken is promised to be the strength of the chosen. He who wings the unerring bolt will give to his redeemed the wings of eagles; he who shakes the earth with his voice will terrify the enemies of his saints, and give his children peace. Why are we weak when we have divine strength to flee to? Why are we troubled when the Lord's own peace is ours? Jesus, the mighty God, is our strength; let us put him on and go forth to our service. Jesus, our blessed Lord, is also our peace; let us repose in him this day, and end our fears. What a blessing to have him for our strength and peace both now and for ever!

That same God who rides upon the storm in days of tempest will also rule the hurricane of our tribulation, and send us, before long, days of peace. We shall have strength for storms, and songs for fair weather. Let us begin to sing at once unto God our strength and our peace. Away, dark thoughts! Up, faith and hope!

'*It shall come to pass, that at evening time it shall be light*' (Zechariah 14:7).

It is a surprise that it should be so; for all things threaten that a evening time it will be dark. God works in a way so much above our fears and hopes that we are greatly amazed, and are led to praise his sovereign grace. No, it will not be with us as our hearts are prophesying: the dark will not deepen into midnight, but it will suddenly brighten into day. Never let us despair. In the worst time let us trust in the Lord who turns the darkness of the shadow of death into the morning. When the tale of bricks is double Moses appears, and when tribulation abounds it is nearest its end.

This promise should assist our patience. The light may not fully come till our hopes are quite spent by waiting all day to no purpose. To the wicked the sun goes down while it is still day; to the righteous the sun rises when it is almost night. May we not with patience wait for that heavenly light, which may be long in coming, but is sure to prove itself well worth waiting for?

Come, my soul, take up thy parable and sing to him who will bless thee in life and in death, in a manner surpassing all that nature has ever seen when at its best.

'And even to your old age I am he; and even to hoar hairs will I carry you: I have made, and I will bear; even I will carry, and will deliver you' (Isaiah 46:4).

Here is a promise for our aged friends; yes, and for us all, as age creeps over us. Let us live long enough, and we shall all have hoar hairs; therefore we may as well enjoy this promise by the foresight of faith.

When we grow old our God will still be the I AM, always remaining the same. Hoar hairs tell of our decay, but he does not decay. When we cannot carry a burden, and can hardly carry ourselves, the Lord will carry us. Even as in our young days he carried us like lambs in his bosom, so will he in our years of infirmity.

He made us, and he will care for us. When we become a burden to our friends, and a burden to ourselves, the Lord will not shake us off, but rather he will take us up and carry and deliver us more fully than ever. In many cases the Lord gives his servants a long and calm evening. They worked hard all day and wore themselves out in their Master's service, and so he said to them, 'Now rest in anticipation of that eternal Sabbath which I have prepared for you'. Let us not dread old age. Let us grow old graciously, since the Lord himself is with us in fullness of grace.

The Treasury of
the New Testament

Jesus

'And she shall bring forth a son, and thou shalt call his name Jesus: for he shall save his people from their sins' (Matthew 1:21).

Bernard has delightfully said that the name of Jesus is honey in the mouth, melody in the ear, and joy in the heart. I rejoice in that expression on my own account, for it gives me my share of the delight, and leads me to hope that, while I am speaking, the sweetness of the precious name of Jesus may fill my own mouth. Here also is a portion for you who are listening: it is melody in the ear. If my voice should be harsh, and my words discordant, you will still have music of the choicest order, for the name itself is essential melody, and my whole sermon will ring with its silver note. May both speaker and hearer join in the third word of Bernard's sentence, and may we all find it to be joy in our hearts, a jubilee within our souls. Jesus is the way to God, therefore will we preach him; he is the truth, therefore will we hear of him; he is the life, therefore shall our hearts rejoice in him.

So inexpressibly fragrant is the name of Jesus that it imparts a delicious perfume to everything which comes in connection with it. Our thoughts will turn this morning to the first use of the name in connection with our Lord, when the child who was yet to be born was named Jesus. Here we find everything suggestive of comfort. The person to whom that name was first revealed was Joseph, a carpenter, a humble man, a working man, unknown and undistinguished save by the justice of his character. It is not, therefore, a title to be monopolized by the ears of princes, sages, priests, warriors, or men of wealth: it is a name to be made a household word among common people. He is the people's Christ; for of old it was said of him, 'I have exalted one chosen out of the people'.

There is consolation in the messenger who made known that name to Joseph; for it was the angel of the Lord who, in the visions of the night, whispered that charming name into his ear; and henceforth angels are in league with men, and gather to one standard, moved by the same watchword as ourselves – the name of Jesus. Did God send the name by an angel, and did the angel delight to come with it? Then is there a bond of sympathy between us and angelic spirits, and we are come this day not only 'to the general assembly and church of the firstborn', but 'to an innumerable company of angels', by whom that name is regarded with reverent love.

The angel spoke to Joseph in a dream: that name is so soft and sweet that it breaks no man's rest, but rather yields a peace unrivalled, the peace of God. With such a dream Joseph's sleep was more blessed than his waking. The name has evermore this power, for, to those who know it, it unveils a glory brighter than dreams have ever imagined. The name of Jesus brings before our minds a vision of glory in the latter days when Jesus will reign from pole to pole, and yet another vision of glory unutterable when his people are with him where he is. The name of Jesus was sweet at the first, because of the words with which it was accompanied; for they were meant to remove perplexity from Joseph's mind, and some of them ran thus: 'Fear not'. Let but the sinner hear of 'the Saviour', and he rises out of the deadly lethargy of his hopelessness, and, looking upward, he sees a reconciled God, and fears no longer. Especially, brothers, this name is full of rare delights when we meditate upon the infinite preciousness of the person to whom it was assigned. We have no common Saviour, for neither earth nor heaven could produce his equal. He bears our nature, but not our corruption; he was made in the likeness of sinful flesh, but yet in his flesh there is no sin. This Holy One is the Son of God, and yet he is the Son of man: this surpassing excellence of nature makes his name most precious.

I shall ask for the exercise of your patience while I consider seven things in reference to this transporting name. It is an ointment poured out, and its scent is varied so as to contain the essence of all fragrances.

A name divinely ordered and expounded

According to the text, the angel brought a message from the Lord, and said, 'Thou shalt call his name Jesus'. It is a name which, like him who bears it, has come down from heaven. Our Lord has other names of office and relationship, but this is specially and peculiarly his own name. Rest assured, therefore, that it is *the best name* that he could bear. God would not have given him a name of secondary value, or about which there would be a trace of dishonour. The name is the highest, brightest, and noblest of names; it is the glory of our Lord to be a Saviour. To the best that was ever born of woman God has given the best name that any son could bear. JESUS is *the most appropriate name* that our Lord could receive. Of this we are quite certain, for the Father knew all about him, and could name him well. He knows much more about the Lord Christ than all saints and angels put together, for 'No man knoweth the Son but the Father'. The Father knew him to perfection, and he names him Jesus. We may be sure, then, that our Lord is most of all a Saviour. Since infinite wisdom has selected it, we may be sure that it is *a name which must be true*, and must be verified by facts of no mean order. God, who cannot be under a mistake, calls him Jesus, a Saviour. Neither will God refuse to accept the work which he has done, since by the gift of that name he has commissioned him to save sinners. When we plead the name of Jesus before God, we bring him back his own word, and appeal to him by his own act and deed. He is not a Saviour of our own setting up, but God the ever-lasting Father has set him forth as our deliverer and saviour.

It is a name which the Holy Spirit explains, for he tells us the reason for the name of Jesus – 'For he shall save his people from their sins'. 'Saviour' is the meaning of the name, but it has a fuller sense hidden within, for in its Hebrew form it means 'the salvation of the Lord', or 'the Lord of salvation', or 'the Saviour'. The angel interprets it, 'he shall save', and the word for 'he' is very emphatic. According to many scholars, the divine name, the incommensu-rable title of the Most High, is contained in 'Joshua', the Hebrew form of 'Jesus', so that in full the word means 'Jehovah Saviour', and in brief it signifies 'Saviour'. It is given to our Lord because 'he saves' –not according to any temporary and common salvation, from enemies and troubles, but he saves from spiritual enemies, and specially from sins. Joshua of old was a saviour, Gideon was a saviour, David was a saviour; but the title is given to our Lord above all others because he is a Saviour in a sense in which no one else is or can be – he saves his people from their sins. The Jews were looking for a Saviour; they expected one who would break the Roman yoke, and save them from being under bondage to a foreign power, but our divine Lord came not for such a purpose: he came to be a Saviour of a more spiritual sort, and to break quite another yoke, by saving his people from their sins.

The word 'save' is very rich in meaning; its full and exact force can hardly be given in English words. Jesus is salvation in the sense of deliverance and also in that of preservation. The original word means to preserve, to keep, to protect from danger, and to secure. Jesus brings a great salvation, or as Paul says 'so great salvation', as if he felt that he could never estimate its greatness (Hebrews 2:3); he also speaks of it as 'eternal salvation' (Hebrews 5:9), even as Isaiah said, 'Israel shall be saved in the Lord with an everlasting salvation'. Glorious beyond measure is the name 'Jesus' as it is divinely expounded to us, for by that very exposition the eternal God guarantees the success of the Saviour.

He shall save his people from their sins; and this is for all time, since he always has a people, and these people evermore need to be saved from their sins. Let us be glad that we have such a Saviour, and that the name of Jesus retains all the sweetness and power it ever had, and shall retain it till all the chosen people are saved, and then for ever and ever.

Moreover, in addition to expounding this name, the Holy Spirit, through the evangelist Matthew, has been pleased to refer us to the synonym of it, and so to give us its meaning by comparison. Let me read you the next verses. 'Now all this was done, that it might be fulfilled which was spoken of the Lord by the prophet, saying, Behold, a virgin shall be with child, and shall bring forth a son, and they shall call his name Emmanuel, which being interpreted is, God with us.' If when our Lord was born and named 'Jesus' the old prophecy which said that he would be called Emmanuel was fulfilled, it follows that the name 'Jesus' bears a meaning tantamount to that of 'Emmanuel', and that its virtual meaning is 'God with us'. Indeed, brothers, he is Jesus, the Saviour, because he is Emmanuel, God with us; and as soon as he was born, and so became Emmanuel, the incarnate God, He became by that very fact Jesus, the Saviour. By coming down from heaven into the earth, and taking upon himself our nature, he bridged the otherwise bridgeless gulf between God and man; by suffering in that human nature and imparting through his divine nature an infinite efficacy to those sufferings he removed that which would have destroyed us, and brought us everlasting life and salvation. Our Saviour is *God*, and therefore able; he is God *with us*, and therefore pitiful; he is divine and therefore infinitely wise; but he is human, and therefore full of compassion.

This, then, is our first head; this charming name of Jesus lets us know the very heart of God in reference to his Son: why he sent him, what he meant him to be and to do, and in what manner he would glorify him.

A name given by man

Although this name was thus chosen by God, our Lord was actually called by the name of Jesus by man. 'She (Mary) shall bring forth a son, and thou (Joseph) shalt call his name Jesus.' The God of heaven by his angel appoints the child's name, but his reputed father must announce it. Those who are taught by God joyfully recognize that Christ is salvation, and without a question give him the well-beloved name of Jesus, the Saviour.

Here note that the name Jesus, Saviour, was given to our Lord by two simple hearts as soon as ever he was revealed to them. They only needed to be told who he was, and what he had come for, how he was born, and what was the object of his incarnation, and they at once accepted the divine message, and named the babe by the name of Jesus. And, brethren, all of us to whom Christ is revealed at all, call him Jesus the Saviour. There are many who think they know our Lord, but since they only speak of him as a prophet, a teacher, or a leader, and do not care for him as a Saviour, we are clear that they are in ignorance as to his chief character. They do not know his first name, his personal name. The Holy Spirit cannot have revealed Christ to any man if that man remains ignorant of his saving power. He who does not know him as Jesus, the Saviour, does not know him at all. Certain anti-Christian Christians are craftily extolling Christ that they may smite Jesus: I mean that they cry up Jesus as Messiah, sent by God, to exhibit a grand example and supply a pure code of morals, but they cannot endure Jesus as a Saviour, redeeming us by his blood, and by his death delivering us from sin. I am not sure that they follow his example of holy living, but they are very loud in extolling it, and all with the purpose of drawing off men's thoughts from the chief character and main object of our Lord's sojourn among us, namely, the deliverance of his people from sin. If men knew our Lord they would call him Jesus the Saviour, and regard him not merely as a good man, a great teacher, a noble exemplar, but as the Saviour of sinners.

Now, Joseph and Mary not only believed, so as to give the young child the name in their own minds, but in due time they took him up to the temple and presented him according to the law, and there publicly his name was called Jesus. All hearts to whom God commits his Christ should publicly own him in the most solemn manner according to his ordinance, and should desire in all proper places to confess him as the Saviour. The infant Christ was committed to the care of Joseph and Mary, to nurse and protect. Wonder of wonders, that *he* should need a guardian who is the Preserver of men and the Shepherd of his saints! In his feebleness as a babe he needed parental care. Now in a certain sense Christ is committed to the keeping of all his people. We are to preserve his Gospel in the world, to maintain his truth, and to publish his salvation, and therefore we are bound to bear this testimony, that he is Jesus, the Saviour of sinners. This we must make very prominent. Others shall say what they please about him, and if they speak well of his character in any respect we will be glad that they do it, however little they may know; but this is our peculiar testimony, that our Lord saves from sin. If he is anything he is Jesus, the Saviour; we know him best by that name. He is righteous and loves righteousness, but he is first known to men as the friend of sinners. He is the faithful and true witness, the prince of the kings of the earth, but his first work is to save; after that he teaches and rules his saved ones.

As Emmanuel, God with us, his very incarnation made him Jesus, the Saviour of men: but what shall I say of him now that beyond his incarnation we have his atonement, and above his atonement his resurrection, and beyond that his ascension, and, to crown all, his perpetual intercession? How grandly does the title befit him now that he is able to save them to the uttermost that come unto God by him, seeing he ever liveth to make intercession for them!

A name typically worn by another, but now reserved for him alone

There had been a Jesus before our Jesus. I allude to Joshua, and you know that in our version the name Jesus is used twice where Joshua is really meant. The first is Acts 7:4–5, where we read of the fathers who entered in with Jesus into the possession of the Gentiles, evidently meaning Joshua; and the second is Hebrews 4:8, 'If Jesus had given them rest'. Joshua is the Hebrew form and Jesus the Greek form, but Jesus and Joshua are the same word. There was one, then, of old, who bore this famous name of Jesus, or Joshua, and was a type of our Jesus. What did Joshua do? When Moses could not lead the people into Canaan, Joshua did it; and so our Jesus accomplishes what the law never could have done. Joshua overcame the enemies of God's people: though they were very many and very strong, and had cities walled to heaven and chariots of iron, yet in the name of Jehovah, as captain of the Lord's host, Joshua smote them. Just so, our glorious Joshua smites our sins and all the powers of darkness, and utterly destroys our spiritual enemies. Before his Amalek is smitten, Jericho falls, and Canaanites are put to rout, while he gives us to triumph in every place. Moreover, Joshua conquered an inheritance for Israel, took them across the Jordan, settled them in a land that flowed with milk and honey, and gave to each tribe and to each man to stand in his lot which God had ordained for him. Precisely this is what our Jesus does, only our inheritance is more divine, and on each one of us it is more surely entailed. Though Joshua could not give to the people the heavenly rest of the highest kind, yet he gave them rest most pleasant to them, so that every man sat under his own vine and fig tree, none making him afraid; but our glorious Joshua has given us infinite, eternal rest, for he is our peace, and they that know him have entered into rest. Joshua, the son of Nun, caused the people to serve the Lord all his days, but he could not save the nation from their sins, for after his death they grievously went astray: our Joshua preserves to himself a people zealous for good works, for he ever liveth and is able to keep them from falling. No more does Joshua lift sword or spear on behalf of Israel, but Jesus still rides out, conquering and to conquer, and all his people have victory through his blood. Well is his name called Jesus.

We read of another Jesus in the books of Ezra and Zechariah.

The form which the word there takes is Jeshua or Joshua. He was the high priest who came at the head of the people on their return from Babylon. He is spoken of by the prophet Zechariah in terms which make him a fit representative of each of us. But Jesus of Nazareth is now the only high priest; and having presented his one sacrifice for ever, he remains a priest according to the power of an endless life. He heads the march from Babylon, and he leads his people back to Jerusalem.

The name of Jesus was not at all uncommon among the Jews. Josephus mentions no less than twelve people of the name of Jesus. Salvation of a certain kind was so longed for by the Jews that their eagerness was seen in their children's names. Their little ones were by their hopes named as saviours, but saviours they were not. How common are nominal saviours! 'Lo here,' they say, 'here is a saviour'; 'Lo, there,' they cry, 'another saviour.' These have the name but not the power, and now, according to the text, Jesus Christ has engrossed the title for himself. His name shall be called Jesus, for he alone is a Prince and a Saviour, and truly saves his people from their sins. 'Look unto me and be ye saved, all ye ends of the earth, for I am God, and beside me there is none else.'

A name identifying our Lord with his people

'Thou shalt call his name Jesus,' for that name declares his relation to his people. It is to them that he is a Saviour. He would not be Jesus if he did not have a people: he could not be, for there could be no Saviour if there were none to be saved, and there could be no Saviour from sin if there were no sinners. His name has no meaning apart from his people.

'He shall save his people.' It does not say God's people, for then it would have been understood as meaning only the Jews — or it would have been supposed to refer to some good and holy people who belonged to God, apart from the Mediator. 'He shall save *his* people' — those who are his own, and personally belong to him. These are evidently a very special people, a people set apart as Christ's own treasure; they are a people that belong to God incar-

85

nate – Emmanuel's people. These he saves. Who are they but his elect, whom his Father gave him before the earth was? Who are they but those whose names are engraved on the palms of his hands, and written on his heart? Who are they but the numbered sheep that will be required at his hands by the great Father, that he should render them back, saying, 'I have kept those whom thou hast given me, for they are thine.'

'He shall save his people.' Do you not see that this name of Jesus is an election name after all? It has a special bearing upon a chosen people; it has a ring of sovereignty about it, and is all the sweeter because of this to those who see in their own salvation an exhibition of distinguishing grace.

Now the question arises, who are his people? We are eager to know who they are; and we are glad to find that his people, be they who they may, need to be saved, and will be saved, for it is written, 'He *shall save* his people.' It is not said, 'He shall reward his people for their righteousness,' nor is it promised that he shall 'save them from becoming sinners', but 'He shall *save* his people from their sins'. Do you want saving, brothers? Has the Holy Spirit taught you that you need salvation? Let your hearts be encouraged! This is the character of all his people; he never had a chosen one who could do without washing in the Saviour's blood. If you are righteous in yourself you are not one of his people. If you were never sick in soul you are none of the folk that the Great Physician has come to heal; if you were never guilty of sin you are none of those whom he has come to deliver from sin. If you feel yourselves to need saving then cast yourselves upon him, for such as you are he came to save.

Notice, yet again, the very gracious but startling fact that our Lord's connection with his people lies in the direction of their sins. If they had never sinned they would never have required a Saviour, and there would have been no name of Jesus known on earth. As Martin Luther says, he never gave himself for our righteousness, but he did give himself for our sins. Sin is a horrible evil, a deadly poison, yet it is this which gives Jesus his title when he overcomes it. The first link between my soul and Christ is not my goodness but my badness; not my merit, but my misery; not my standing but my falling; not my riches but my need. O you sinners – I mean real sinner, not you that call yourselves so because you are told you are such, but you who feel yourselves to be guilty before God – here is good news for you. O you self-condemned sinners, who feel that if you ever get salvation Jesus must bring it to you and be the beginning and the end of it, I pray you rejoice in this dear, precious, blessed name, for Jesus has come to save you, even you. Go to him as sinners, call him 'Jesus', and cry, 'O Lord Jesus, be Jesus to me, for I need your salvation'. Do not doubt that he will fulfil his own name and exhibit his power in you. Only confess to him your sin, and he will save you from it. Only believe in him, and he will be your salvation.

A name which indicates his main work

Why do men write lives of Christ who know nothing about his main business and object? Why do some preach about Christ who do not know the very essence and heart of him? There is no knowing our Lord, if he is not known as a Saviour; for he is that or nothing. Those who fall short of his salvation do not even know his name; how, then should they know his person? His name is not called Jesus because he is our exemplar, though indeed he is perfection itself, and we long to tread in his footsteps; but his name is called Jesus because he has come to save that which is lost. He is Christ, too, or the anointed, but then he is Christ Jesus; that is to say, it is as a Saviour that he is anointed. He is nothing if not a Saviour.

Now, Jesus saves his people from sin: for, first, he does it by taking all the sins of his people upon himself. Do you think that a strong expression? It is warranted by the Scriptures. 'The Lord hath laid on him the iniquity of us all.' Christ's shoulders bore the guilt of his people, and because he took their load his people are free, and have henceforth no burden of sin to weigh them down. He saves his people through his personal substitution, by standing in their stead and suffering in their place. There is no other way of salvation but by his vicarious sufferings and death.

Then he saves them by bearing the penalty due to their sin. 'The chastisement of our peace was upon him, and with his stripes we are healed.' 'He was made a curse for us.' 'Christ also hath suffered for us.' He died, 'the just for the unjust, to bring us to God'. He bore the wrath of God which was due to us. He has taken the sin and paid the penalty, and now cavillers come in and falsely say that we teach that a man is to believe the dogma of atonement and then he is saved, and may live as he likes. They know better; they know that they misrepresent us, for we always teach that this great work of substitution and penalty-bearing by Christ works in the person who partakes of it benefits, love to God, gratitude to Christ, and consequent hatred of all sin; *and this change of heart is the very core and essence of salvation.* This is how Christ saves his people from their sin – by rescuing them, by the force of his love, out of the power, tyranny, and dominion of sins, which hitherto had the mastery over them. I knew what it was to strive against sin as a moral person, seeking to overcome it, but I found myself mastered by sin, like Samson when his hair was lost, and the Philistines bound him; but since I have believed in Jesus I find motives for being holy which are more influential with me than any I knew before; I find weapons with which to fight my sin that I never knew how to handle before, and a new strength has been given me by the Holy Spirit. 'This is the victory that overcometh the world, even our faith'; this is the power which drives out the vipers of sin from the soul – the precious blood of Jesus. He who has believed in Jesus as his expiation and atonement becomes thereby, through the power of the Holy Spirit, renewed in heart; he has fresh objects set him, fresh motives sway him, and thus Jesus saves his people from their sins.

A name justified by facts

Many a child has had a grand name, and his life has contradicted it. I recollect a grave on which there is the name of a child, 'Sacred to the memory of Methuselah Coney, who died aged six months'. Many other names are equally inappropriate, and are proved to be so in the course of years. But this Jesus is a Saviour, a true Jesus. He bears a name which he well deserves. Come to the Christ and see there the many that once rioted in sin, and rolled in the mire, but they are washed, but they are sanctified, and now they rejoice in holiness. Who purified them? Who but Jesus? He that saves his people from their sins has saved them. When he comes from heaven, it will be seen that he has saved his church, his people, from their sins.

Christ's personal name for ever

It is the name his father and mother gave him – the child Jesus. We also belong to his family; for he that believes in him is his father, and mother, and sister, and brother, and that most dear and familiar name by which he was known at home is ever in our mouths. He is the Lord, and we worship him; but he is Jesus, and we love him. It is the name which moves our affections, and fires our souls. Jesus is his death name – 'Jesus of Nazareth, King of the Jews' was written on his cross. That is his resurrection name. That is his Gospel name, which we preach. It is the name which Peter preached to the Gentiles when he said, 'This is Jesus of Nazareth by whom is preached to you the remission of sins.' And this, beloved, is his heaven name. They sing to him there as Jesus. See how it concludes the Bible. Read the Revelation, and read its songs, and see how they worship Jesus the Lamb of God. Let us go and tell of his name; let us continually meditate upon it; let us love it henceforth and for ever. Amen.

Christ's word with you

'Come unto me, all ye that labour and are heavy laden, and I will give you rest.' (Matthew 11:28).

One is struck with the personality of this text. There are two persons in it, 'ye' and 'me' – that is to say, the labouring one and the

89

tender Saviour who entreats him to come that he may find rest. It is most important, if we wish to see the way of peace clearly, to understand that we must each one come personally to Jesus for rest – 'Come unto me, all ye that labour' – and that coming on our part must be to a personal Christ. In effect he says, 'Come yourselves to me. Come not through sponsors, nor through men whom you choose to call your priests, not through the petitions of ministers and teachers, but come yourselves, for yourselves.' The quarrel is between you and God, and this quarrel can only be made up by your approaching the Lord through a Mediator; it would be folly for you to ask another to come to the Mediator for you: you must trust in him yourself. Personal faith is indispensable to salvation.

But the personality of Christ is equally clearly brought out in our text. Jesus says, 'Come unto me' – not to anybody else, but 'to me'. He does not say, 'Come to hear a sermon about me,' but 'come to me'. He does not say, 'Come to sacraments, which will teach you something about me,' but 'come to me' – to my work and person. You will observe that no one is put between you and Christ. The text is, 'Come unto me, all ye that labour and are heavy laden' – not to somebody that will stand between you and me, but 'Come to me at once, and without a go-between'. Come to Jesus directly, even to Jesus himself. You do want a mediator between yourselves and God, but you do not want a mediator between yourselves and Jesus. Christ Jesus is the Mediator between you and the Father; but you need no one to stand between you and Christ. To him we may look at once, with unveiled face, guilty as we are. To him we may come, just as we are, without anyone to recommend us, or plead for us, or make a bridge for us to Jesus. We are to come directly to the Lord Jesus Christ, the Son of God, whom God has ordained to be the way of access. I shall fail at this time in setting forth the Gospel if I lead anybody to think that he can get salvation by going to church, or going to a minister. You, as you are, are to come to Christ as he is, and the promise is that on your coming to him he will give you rest. What a blessing it will be if those who have no rest in themselves should find rest at once in Jesus while yet this sermon calls them.

Why not? Jesus says to you, 'Come to me'. Your answer to him, if it is 'Yes, Lord, I come', will be the means of bringing peace to your heart from this time forth and for evermore.

I want at this time to set forth the glory of the Lord Jesus Christ, who sends this pressing personal invitation to every labouring and heavy-laden one in this place. I wish that I knew how to preach. I have tried to do so for thirty years or so, but I am only now beginning to learn the art. Oh that one knew how to set forth Christ so that men perceived his beauty, and fell in love with him at first sight! Oh, Spirit of God, make it so *now*. If men knew the grandeur of his Gospel – the joy, the peace, the happiness which comes of being a Christian, they would run to him.

The value of the boon
Rest of the heart is worth more than all California
To be at peace – to be no more tossed up and down in the soul – to be secure, peaceful, joyful, happy, is worth mountains of diamonds. Peace comes not with property, but with content. It is this boon which, for value, outshines the pearls and rubies which deck an Indian queen, which Jesus promises to give to all that come to him for it. Oh rare peace which comes from the Prince of peace!

It is practically helpful in all the affairs of life
Other things being equal, there is nobody so fit to run the race of life as the man who is unloaded of his cares and enjoys peace of mind. I have known a man losing money on the market step aside, and, getting into a quiet place, breathe a prayer to God, and come back calm and composed; and whereas before in his distraction he was ready to make bad bargains, plunge into speculation, and lose terribly, he has come back rested and peaceful, and has been in a fit frame for dealing with his fellow-men. When a man is afraid to die, he may well be afraid to live. He who could not look death in the face – that could not look God in the face – is a man who has a latent weakness about him that will rob him of force and courage in the heat of the battle. I commend to you, men and brothers, in this

busy London, the precious boon of my text called 'rest', because it is not only a preparation for the world to come, but for the life that now is.

It is not found anywhere else but in Christ
It is rest to the man's entire spiritual being.

Conscience: Conscience troubles us till Jesus speaks it into rest. Conscience looks back and cries, 'Things are not right. You were wrong here, and wrong altogether: there is no rest for you.' Conscience keeps a daybook, and writes with heavy pen a gloomy record, which we read with alarm. Now, Jesus promises to those who come to him a peaceful conscience, which he will give through pardoning all the past, through changing the current of our ideas in the present, and through helping us to avoid in the future the faults into which we fell in the past.

Mind: It is a grand thing to have rest of conscience, but then we have minds, and minds are troublous things. In these days of doubt it is not easy for a mind to get an anchorage, and keep it. Many are searching for something to believe, or, at least, they long to be quite sure that it would be the right thing *not* to believe. Minds are tossed about like ships at sea, or birds caught in a fierce gale. My mind was once in that state – drifted, carried along I knew not whither; for a while I believed nothing, till it last it came to this – that I thought my own existence might be, after all, a mere thought. Having a practical vein in my character, I sat down and laughed at my own dreams of non-existence, for I felt that I *did* exist. Up from the depths of doubt and unbelief rose the feeling that there must be something sure. I cast my soul at Jesus's feet, and I rested, and I am now perfectly content in mind. Thousands of us can say, 'We know whom we have believed, and are persuaded that he is able to keep that which we have committed to him'; therefore we cannot leave the Gospel. No new doctrines, no novelties, no scepticisms, no fresh information can disturb us now: at least, they can only breathe a surface-ruffling; all is calm in the soul's deeps. Having found rest of intellect in the doctrine of Jesus, there we will stay till death and heaven, or the second advent, solves all riddles.

Heart: But then we have hearts. Men that have great, all-embracing hearts need a rest for their love. What a cause of trouble this heart of ours is, for it often clings to that which is unworthy of it; and we are deceived and disappointed, and heart-break crushes us. The tempting fruit, like the apple of Sodom, crumbles into ashes in our hand. Here then is rest and remedy for heart palpitations and the anguish of the breast. Let a man love Jesus and he will crave no other love, for this will fill his soul to the brim.

The largeness of the Saviour's heart
See the people whom he invites to come to him. None but a man of great soul would keep such company. If we want to be merry, we choose merry company. Some folks I should be glad to be in heaven with, but I could dispense with their company here: for ten minutes with them on earth is enough to make one wretched. Only a generous spirit would say, 'Come to me, all you that are downcast – all you that are desponding – all you that are broken-hearted'. Yet that is exactly what the text says. Christ courts the company of the sorrowful, and invites those who are ill at ease to approach him. What a heart of love he must have! The love of my Master's heart is so great, and the sympathy of his nature with man is so deep, that if all should come that ever laboured or ever sorrowed, he would not be exhausted by the sympathy, but would still be able to give them rest in himself.

He says, 'Come at once!'
There is a notion in some people's minds that they cannot believe in Christ till they are better. Christ does not want your betterness. Will you only go to the physician when you feel better? Then you are foolish indeed, for you do not want the physician when you are getting better. The best time to apply to a physician is when you are

as bad as you can be; and the time to come to Jesus is when you are so bad that you cannot be worse. You had better come just as you are. If you cannot come *with* a broken heart, come *for* a broken heart. If you cannot come *with* faith, come *for* faith. If you cannot come repenting, come and ask the Lord to give you repentance. Come empty-handed, bankrupt, ruined, condemned, and you will find rest. Oh, you that have written out your own sentence, and have said, 'I shall perish; there is no pardon for me': come to Jesus, for – depths of mercy! – there is pardon even for you. Only come to the Saviour, and he will give you rest.

He promises this rest to all who come to him

My Master stakes his credit upon every case that comes to him. He has already given rest to thousands, to millions; and he promises to each one that comes to him that he will give rest to him. He says, 'Him that cometh to me I will in no wise cast out.' Each heavy-laden one must and shall find rest if he will come to Jesus, or else the Redeemer's promise is not true.

The blessedness of his power

Our Lord Jesus is able to give peace to all that labour and are heavy laden. He has not outrun his power in the promise that he has given. He is conscious that within himself there resides a power which will be able to give peace to every conscience.

Notice there is no limiting clause. Whoever of woman born that labours and is heavy laden, and will come to Christ, must have rest; and Christ has said it because he can give it. There are desperate cases among the myriads of troubled hearts, but no single one is too far gone for Jesus. You have read the story of John Bunyan in *Grace Abounding*. Was there ever a poor wretch that was dragged about by the devil more than John was? For five years and more he could not call his soul his own. He did not dare to sleep, because he was afraid he would wake up in hell; and all day long he was troubled, and fretted, and worried with this and that and the other. I am sure such a case as that would have been given up by men; but when

Jesus took it in hand John Bunyan found perfect rest; and his blessed *Pilgrim's Progress* remains a proof of the joy of heart which the poor tinker found when he came to rest in Christ. Now, if within these walls there is a case in which poverty combines with sickness and disease, and if that poverty and disease are the result of vice, and if that vice has been carried on for many years, and if the entire man is now depressed and despondent, yet the Lord Jesus can give rest. It does not matter how black or horrible your condition is, if you believe in Jesus you will be saved. As far as this trouble of soul is concerned, and as far as the venom of sin in your nature is concerned, you will be healed. You will be started again in life by a power that will cause you to be born again, so that you will be as though you were a little child commencing life again only under happier skies and holier influences. Jesus is able to give rest. He is willing to cause joy. Doubt no more.

Jesus *speaks* thus *without reserve* because he is conscious of power; for note this: Jesus Christ is God, and he that made men's hearts can make them all anew. This blessed God took upon himself our nature and became man, and being found in fashion as a man he took men's grief and sin upon him, and went up to the cross loaded with it, and there suffered in our room and stead, to make expiation for our guilt. There is such merit in his blood that no sin can ever overpower it. Oh, sinner, Christ is able to cast your sins into the depths of the sea, so that they will never be mentioned against you any more for ever, and thus he will give you serenest rest.

My Master knows that he can save you, for *he had reckoned up every possible case before he spoke so positively*. His prescient eye discerned all men that have ever lived, or that ever will live, and he perceives you, dear friend, whom nobody else knows. You up in the corner there, whom nobody understands, not even yourself – he understands you, and he is able to give rest to your eccentric mind. He meant this promise to ring down the ages till it reached you. Will not *you* come at once and test that power? Oh that the Holy Spirit may incline you to do so!

The simplicity of this invitation

What is the way of salvation? If any minister replies, 'I should want a week or two to explain it to you,' he does not know the way of salvation; because the way of salvation which we need must suit a dying man, an illiterate man, and a guilty man, or else it will be unavailing in many cases.

Our Lord Jesus Christ proves how willing he is to save sinners by making the method of grace so easy. He says, 'Come to me'. 'Well,' says someone, 'how am I to come?' Come anyhow. If you can run, come running; if you can walk, come walking; if you can creep, come creeping; if you can only limp, come limping – come anyhow, so long as you come to Jesus.

'But what is coming to him?' says someone. 'We are not to come to him with our persons, or with our legs and feet by a visible motion. How, then, can we come to him?' Listen, you friends in the front gallery, how can I come to you and yet stand here? Why, by thinking about you, knowing about you, and then confiding my thoughts to you, as I am now doing. If you over there are a businessman, I resolve in my mind that I will commit my affairs into your hands; and in so doing I have mentally come to you. We are to do with our Lord Jesus just what we do with a physician. We are very ill; it is a bad case. We hear that a certain eminent doctor has great skill in one particular disease; so at once we go to him. Our physical going is not so much required as our mental resort to him, by putting our case into his hands. We say to him, 'I place myself entirely in your hands because I have faith in your skill. You cured my mother of this disease; you cured my brother; and I believe you can cure *me*.' Such is faith in Christ. If this is a genuine surrender, and a hearty confidence, you are already a healed man. Your power to trust Christ is evidence of spiritual sanity: you would not have been able to trust the blessed Jesus if a sound work of restoration had not already commenced in you.

'Oh,' says someone, 'do I understand, then, that if I trust Christ, I may do as I like?' Stop, stop. I never said that. Here is a ship which cannot get into the haven. The pilot comes on board. The captain goes to the helm, or gives orders as to steering the vessel, and at once the pilot objects that they are not trusting to him. 'Yes I am,' says the captain, 'and I expect you to get me into harbour, for you promised to do so.' 'Of course I did promise,' replies the pilot, 'but then it was understood that I should take charge of the ship for the time being. Unless you trust me I can do nothing, and the proof that you trust me is that you obey my orders.' Now, then, trust Jesus, so as to be obedient to him, and he will pilot you safely. Yield yourself up to follow his example, to imitate his spirit, and obey his commands, and you are a saved man. Give yourself up to Jesus, renounce your sins, forsake your old habits, live as Christ will enable you to live, and immediately you will find peace to your soul. You cannot enjoy rest, and yet riot in sin. Oh, that you would come to him while I am speaking, and find instantaneous rest to your souls!

The unselfishness of the Lord Jesus Christ

'Come unto me,' says he, 'and I will *give* you.' That is the Gospel. '*I* will give *you*.' You say, 'Lord, I cannot give you anything.' He does not want anything. Not what you give to God, but what he gives to you, will be your salvation. Will you come and have it? It lies open before you. Jesus wants nothing of you. Suppose you were to become Christ's disciple, and serve him with all your might throughout your life – in what way would that enrich *him*? He has died for you; how can you ever pay him for that? He lives in heaven to plead for you, and he loves you; how can you ever reward him for that? See, then, how the unselfishness of his character comes out in his inviting to come to himself those who cannot benefit him, but must be pensioners on his bounty.

The day is coming when we shall all sigh for rest. We need it badly now, and if we do not have it we are leading a pitiful life. Those poor rich people in the West End that have no Christ, how can they bear their irksome idleness, the satiety and disgust of unenjoyed abundance? These poor people in the East End that have no Christ – what they do without him I cannot tell. Alas for

97

their poverty and suffering, but what are these to their wretchedness in being Christless? Those of us who have all that heart can wish yet feel that we could never be happy if we were not resting in our dear Saviour; how, then, do the starving exist without him? But we shall soon die, and what then? He that is ready to live tomorrow is ready to die tomorrow. There is no need that death should be a jerk in our existence; life ought to run on as a river pursues its way, and widens into the sea. Our existence here should glide into our existence there, but that cannot be unless we get on the right track while we are here. If we are on the right track now, which is believing, loving, fearing, serving, honouring God, we shall go on loving, fearing, honouring God for ever and ever. 'Come', says Christ, 'to me.' What will Jesus say at the judgement day to those who thus come? Why, he will say, 'Come' – 'Come, ye blessed of my Father. Keep on coming. Come, and inherit the kingdom prepared for you from before the foundations of the world.' Ah, my hearers, you will prize this coming when death and eternity are near you.

I am glad to see this great company gathered here, but before I came into this house I felt much heaviness of heart, and it has not gone from me even now. To stand here and look into familiar faces from Sunday to Sunday is infinitely more pleasant than to look upon so many, most of whom I have never seen before; for you cause me new anxieties that I may do good to you also. This was my thought: 'I shall see them all again at the judgement day, and I shall be accountable as to whether I preached the Gospel to them with all my heart.' I speak in the name of God, and if you think I do, and believe that God has sent me, then I beseech you to lay hold of the truth which has been held up before you. The most important thing a man can do is to attend to that which is most important: your soul is of more importance than your body, and therefore your eternal life ought to secure more attention than your mere temporal existence. He that wishes to live for ever should, at least, consider where he wants to live, with whom he wants to live, and how he can secure happiness in such a life. If there is a God – and that there is a God is written on the very skies – I devoutly desire to have him for my friend. I think, as I look up to the stars, 'I love the God that made those shining worlds, I worship him, I desire to serve him, I wish to be at peace with him.' And what has made me desire to serve him and obey him? Can it be a lie which has done this? Does a lie make a man love God, and desire to serve him? No. It is truth, then, that has made me of obedient heart. The Gospel must be true, or it could not thus put men right with their Creator. O my beloved, trust your Saviour. Lay hold on Jesus. Oh, may Christ lay hold on you at this good hour, and cause you to enter into his rest. Amen and amen.

Lectures to my students

The minister's self-watch

'Take heed unto thyself, and unto the doctrine' (1 Timothy 4:16).

Every workman knows the necessity of keeping his tools in a good state of repair, for 'if the iron be blunt, and he do not whet the edge, then must he put to more strength'. If the workman lose the edge from his adze, he knows that there will be a greater draught upon his energies, or his work will be badly done. Michelangelo, the elect of the fine arts, understood so well the importance of his tools that he always made his own brushes with his own hands, and in this he gives us an illustration of the God of grace, who with special care fashion for himself all true ministers. It is true that the Lord, like Quintin Matsys in the story of the Antwerp well-cover, can work with the faultiest kind of instrumentality, as he does when he occasionally makes very foolish preaching to be useful in conversion; and he can even work without agents, as he does when he saves men without a preacher at all, applying the word directly by his Holy Spirit; but we cannot regard God's absolutely sovereign acts as a rule for our action. He may, in his own absoluteness, do as pleases him best, but we must act as his plainer dispensations instruct us; and one of the facts which is clear enough is this, that the Lord

100

usually adapts means to ends, from which the plain lesson is that we shall do worst when they are most out of trim. This is a practical truth for our guidance, when the Lord makes exceptions, they do but prove the rule.

We are, in a certain sense, our own tools, and therefore must keep ourselves in order. If I want to preach the Gospel, I can only use my own voice; therefore I must train my vocal powers. I can only think with my own brains, and feel with my own heart, and therefore I must educate my intellectual and emotional faculties. I can only weep and agonize for souls in my own renewed nature, therefore I must watchfully maintain the tenderness which was in Christ Jesus. It will be in vain for me to stock my library, or organize societies, or project schemes, if I neglect the culture of myself; for books, and agencies, and systems, are only remotely the instruments of my holy calling; my own spirit, soul, and body are my nearest machinery for sacred service; my spiritual faculties, and my inner life, are my battleaxe and weapons of war. M'Cheyne, writing to a ministerial friend who was travelling with a view to perfecting himself in the German tongue, used language identical with our own:

> I know you will apply hard to German, but do not forget the culture of the inner man – I mean of the heart. How diligently the cavalry officer keeps his sabre clean and sharp; every stain he rubs off with the greatest care. Remember you are God's sword, his instrument – I trust, a chosen vessel unto him to bear his name. In great measure, according to the purity and perfection of the instrument, will be the success. It is not great talents God blesses so much as likeness to Jesus. A holy minister is an awful weapon in the hand of God.

For the herald of the Gospel to be spiritually out of order in his own person is, both to himself and to his work, a most serious calamity; and yet, my brethren, how easily is such an evil produced, and with what watchfulness must it be guarded against! Travelling one day by express from Perth to Edinburgh, on a sudden we came to a dead stop, because a very small screw in one of the engines – every railway locomotive consisting virtually of two engines – had been broken, and when we started again we were obliged to crawl along with one piston-rod at work instead of two. Only a small screw gone, if that had been right the train would have rushed along its iron road, but the absence of that insignificant piece of iron disarranged the whole. A train is said to have been stopped on one of the United States' railways by flies in the grease-boxes of the carriage wheels. The analogy is perfect; a man in all other respects fitted to be useful may by some small defect be exceedingly hindered, or even rendered utterly useless. Such a result is all the more grievous because it is associated with the Gospel, which in the highest sense is adapted to effect the grandest results. It is a terrible thing when the healing balm loses its efficacy through the blunderer who administers it. You all know the injurious effect frequently produced upon water through flowing along lead pipes; even so the Gospel itself, in flowing through men who are spiritually unhealthy, may be debased until it grows injurious to their hearers. It is to be feared that Calvinistic doctrine becomes most evil teaching when it is set forth by men of ungodly lives, and exhibited as if it were a cloak for licentiousness; and Arminianism, on the other hand, with its wide sweep of the offer of mercy, may do most serious damage to the souls of men if the careless tone of the preacher leads his hearers to believe that they can repent whenever they please; and that, therefore, no urgency surrounds the Gospel message. Moreover, when a preacher is poor in grace, any lasting good which may be the result of his ministry will usually be feeble and utterly out of proportion with what might have been expected. Much sowing will be followed by little reaping; the interest upon the talents will be inappreciably small. In two or three of the battles which were lost in the recent American war, the result is said to have been due to the bad gunpowder which was served out by certain shoddy contractors to the army, so that the due effect of a cannonade was not produced. So it may be with us. We may miss our mark, lose our end and aim, and waste our time, through not possessing true vital force within ourselves, or not possessing it in such a degree that God could consistently bless us. Beware of being shoddy preachers.

We must be saved men

It should be one of our first cares that we ourselves should be saved men.

That a teacher of the Gospel should first be a partaker of it is a simple truth, but at the same time a rule of the most weighty importance. We are not among those who accept the apostolic succession of young men simply because they assume it; if their college experience has been vivacious rather than spiritual, if their honours have been connected rather with athletic exercises than with labours for Christ, we demand evidence of another kind than they are able to present to us. No amount of fees paid to learned doctors, and no amount of classics received in return, appear to us to be evidences of a call from above. True and genuine piety is necessary as the first indispensable requisite; whatever 'call' a man may pretend to have, if he has not been called to holiness, he certainly has not been called to the ministry.

'First be trimmed thyself, and then adorn thy brother' say the rabbis. 'The hand that means to make another clean', says Gregory, 'must not itself be dirty.' If your salt is unsavoury, how can you season others? Conversion is a *sine qua non* in a minister. You aspirants to our pulpits 'must be born again'. Nor is the possession of this first qualification a thing to be taken for granted by any man, for there is very great possibility of our being mistaken as to whether we are converted or not. Believe me, it is no child's play to 'make your calling and election sure'. The world is full of counterfeits, and swarms with panderers to carnal self-conceit, who gather around a minister as vultures around a carcass. Our own hearts are deceitful, so that truth lies not on the surface, but must be drawn up from the deepest well. We must search ourselves very anxiously and very thoroughly, lest by any means after having preached to others we ourselves should be castaways.

How horrible to be a preacher of the Gospel and yet to be unconverted! Let each man here whisper to his own inmost soul, 'What a dreadful thing it will be *for me* if I should be ignorant of the power of the truth which I am preparing to proclaim!' Unconverted ministry involves the most unnatural relationships. A graceless pastor is a blind man elected to a professorship of optics, philosophizing upon light and vision, discoursing upon and distinguishing to others the nice shades and delicate blendings of the prismatic colours, while he himself is absolutely in the dark! He is a dumb man elevated to the chair of music; a deaf man fluent upon symphonies and harmonies! He is a mole professing to educate eaglets; a limpet elected to preside over angels. To such a relationship one might apply the most absurd and grotesque metaphors, except that the subject is too solemn. It is a dreadful position for a man to stand in, for he has undertaken a work for which he is totally, wholly, and altogether unqualified, but from the responsibilities of which this unfitness will not screen him, because he wilfully incurred them. Whatever his natural gifts, whatever his mental powers may be, he is utterly out of court for spiritual work if he has no spiritual life; and it is his duty to cease the ministerial office till he has received this first and simplest of qualifications for it.

The unconverted minister is unhappy

Unconverted ministry must be equally dreadful in another respect. If the man has no commission, what a very unhappy position for him to occupy! What can he see in the experience of his people to give him comfort? How must he feel when he hears the cries of penitents; or listens to their anxious doubts and solemn fears? He must be astonished to think that his words should be owned to that end! The word of an unconverted man may be blessed to the conversion of souls, since the Lord, while he disowns him, will still honour his own truth. How perplexed such a man must be when he is consulted concerning the difficulties of mature Christians! In the pathway of experience, in which his own regenerate hearers are led, he must feel himself quite at a loss. How can he listen to their deathbed joys, or join in their rapturous fellowships around the table of their Lord?

In many instances of young men put to a trade which they cannot endure, they have run away to sea sooner than follow an irksome business; but where shall that man flee who is apprenticed for life to this holy calling, and yet is a total stranger to the power of godliness? How can he daily bid men come to Christ, while he himself is a stranger to his dying love? O sirs, surely this must be perpetual slavery. Such a man must hate the sight of a pulpit as much as a galley-slave hates the oar.

The unconverted minister is unserviceable

And how unserviceable such a man must be. He has to guide travellers along a road which he has never trodden, to navigate a vessel along a coast of which he knows none of the landmarks! He is called to instruct others, being himself a fool. What can he be but a cloud with rain, a tree with leaves only. As when the caravan in the wilderness, all athirst and ready to die beneath the broiling sun, comes to the long-desired well, and – horror of horrors – finds it without a drop of water; so when souls thirsting after God come to a graceless ministry, they are ready to perish because the water of life is not to be found. Better abolish pulpits than fill them with men who have no experimental knowledge of what they teach.

The unconverted minister is dangerous

Alas, the unregenerate pastor becomes terribly mischievous too, for of all the causes which create infidelity, ungodly ministers must be ranked among the first. I read the other day that no phase of evil presented so marvellous a power for destruction as the unconverted minister of a parish, with a £1200 organ, a choir of ungodly singers, and an aristocratic congregation. It was the opinion of the writer that there could be no greater instrument for damnation out of hell than that. People go to their place of worship and sit down comfortably, and think they must be Christians, when all the time all that their religion consists in is listening to an orator, having their ears tickled with music, and perhaps their eyes amused with graceful action and fashionable manners; the whole being no better than what they hear and see at the opera – not so good, perhaps, in point of aesthetic beauty, and not an atom more spiritual. Thousands are congratulating themselves, and even blessing God that they are devout worshippers, when at the same time they are living in an unregenerate Christless state, having the form of godliness, but denying the power thereof. He who presides over a system which aims at nothing higher than formalism is far more a servant of the devil than a minister of God.

A formal preacher is mischievous while he preserves his outward equilibrium, but as he is without the preserving balance of godliness, sooner or later he is almost sure to make a trip in his moral character, and what a position he is in then! How is God blasphemed, and the Gospel abused!

The unconverted minister faces a terrible state hereafter
It is terrible to consider what a death must await such a man, and what his after-condition must be! The prophet pictures the king of Babylon going down to hell, and all the kings and princes whom he had destroyed, and whose capitals he had laid waste, rising up from their places in Pandemonium, and greeting the fallen tyrant with the cutting sarcasm, 'Art thou become like unto us?' And cannot you suppose a man who has been a minister, but who has lived without Christ in his heart, going down to hell, and all the imprisoned spirits who used to hear him, and all the ungodly of his parish rising up and saying to him in bitter tones, 'Have you too become as we are? Physician, did you not heal yourself? Are you who claimed to be a shining light cast down into the darkness for ever?' Oh, if one must be lost, let it not be in this fashion! To be lost under the shadow of a pulpit is dreadful, but how much more so to perish from the pulpit itself!

Bunyan's views and Baxter's

There is an awful passage in John Bunyan's treatise *Songs from Hell* which often rings in my ears:

> How many souls have blind priests been the means of destroying by their ignorance? Preaching that was no better for their souls than ratsbane to the body. Many of them, it is to be feared, have whole towns to answer for. Ah, friend, I tell thee, thou that hast taken in hand to preach to the people, it may be thou hast taken in hand thou canst not tell what. Will it not grieve thee to see thy whole parish bellowing after thee into hell, crying out, 'This we have to thank thee for, thou wast afraid to tell us of our sins, lest we should not put meat fast enough into thy mouth! O cursed wretch, who wast not content, blind guide as thou wast, to fall into the ditch thyself, but hast also led us thither with thee.'

Richard Baxter, in his *Reformed Pastor*, amid much other solemn matter, writes as follows:

> Take heed to yourselves let you should be void of that saving grace of God which you offer to others, and be strangers to the effectual working of that Gospel which you preach; and lest, while you proclaim the necessity of a Saviour to the world, your hearts should neglect him, and you should miss of an interest in him and has saving benefits. Take heed to yourselves, lest you perish while you call upon others to take heed of perishing, and lest you famish while you prepare their food. Though there be a promise of shining as stars to those that turn many to righteousness (Daniel 12:3), this is but on supposition that they be first turned to it themselves: such promises are made *caeteris paribus, et suppositis supponendis*. Their own sincerity in the faith is the condition of their glory simply considered, though their great ministerial labours may be a condition of the promise of their greater glory. Many men

107

have warned others that they come not to that place of torment, which yet they hasted to themselves; many a preacher is now in hell, that hath an hundred times called upon his hearers to use the utmost care and diligence to escape it. Can any reasonable man imagine that God should save men for offering salvation to others, while they refused it themselves, and for telling others those truths which they themselves neglected and abused? Many a tailor goes in rags that maketh costly clothes for others; and many a cook scarce licks his fingers, when he hath dressed for others the most costly dishes. Believe it, brethren, God never saved any man for being a preacher, nor because he was an able preacher; but because he was a justified, sanctified man, and consequently faithful in his Master's work. Take heed, therefore, to yourselves first, that you be that which you persuade others to be, and believe that which you persuade them daily to believe, and have heartily entertained that Christ and Spirit which you offer unto others. He that bade you love your neighbours as yourselves, did imply that you should love yourselves and not hate and destroy both yourselves and them.

My brethren, let these weighty sentences have due effect upon you. Surely there can be no need to add more; but let me pray you to examine yourselves, and so make good use of what has been addressed to you.

Our piety must be vigorous

The minister must not be content with being equal with the rank and file of Christians; he must be a mature and advanced believer; for the ministry of Christ has been truly called 'the choicest of his choice, the elect of his election, a church picked out of the church'. If he were called to an ordinary position, and to common work, common grace might perhaps satisfy him, though even then it would be an indolent satisfaction; but being chosen for extraordinary labours, and called to a place of unusual peril, he should be anxious to possess that superior strength which alone is adequate to his station. His pulse of vital godliness must beat strongly and regularly; his eye of faith must be bright, his foot of resolution must be firm; his hand of activity must be quick; his whole inner man must be in the highest degree of sanity. It is said of the Egyptians that they chose their priests from the most learned of their philosophers, and then they esteemed their priests so highly that they chose their kings from them. We require to have for God's ministers the pick of all the Christian host; such men indeed, that if the nation wanted kings they could not do better than elevate them to the throne. Our weakest-minded, most timid, most carnal, and most ill-balanced men are not suitable candidates for the pulpit. There are some works which we should never allot to the invalid or deformed. A man may not be qualified for climbing lofty buildings, his head may be too weak, and elevated work might place him a great danger; but all means let him keep on the ground and find useful occupation where a steady head is less important: there are brethren who have analogous spiritual deficiencies; they cannot be called to service which is conspicuous and elevated because they would be intoxicated with vanity – a vice all too common among ministers, and of all things the least becoming in them, and the most certain to secure them a fall. Should we as a nation be called to defend our hearths and homes, we would not send out our boys and girls with swords and guns to meet the foe; neither may the church send out every fluent novice or inexperienced zealot to plead for the faith. The fear of the Lord must teach the young man wisdom, or he is barred from the pastorate; the grace of God must mature his spirit, or he had better tarry till power be given him from on high.

The highest moral character must be sedulously maintained. Many are disqualified for office in the church who are well enough as simple members. I hold very stern opinions with regard to Christian men who have fallen into gross sin; I rejoice that they may be truly converted, and may be with mingled hope and caution received into the church; but I question, gravely question, whether a man who has grossly sinned should be very readily restored to the pulpit. As John Angell James remarks, 'When a preacher of righteousness has stood in the way of sinners, he should never again open his lips in the great congregation until his repentance is as notorious as his sin'. Let those who have been shorn by the sons of Ammon tarry at Jericho till their beards have grown; this has often been used as a taunt to beardless boys to whom it is evidently inapplicable, but it is an accurate enough metaphor for dishonoured and characterless men, let their age be what it may. Alas, the beard of reputation once shorn is hard to grow again! Open immorality, in most cases, however deep the repentance, is a fatal sign that ministerial graces were never in the man's character. Caesar's wife must be beyond suspicion, and there must be no ugly rumours as to ministerial inconsistency in the past, or the hope of usefulness will be slender. Into the church such fallen ones are to be received as penitents, and into the ministry they may be received if God puts them there; my doubt is not about that, but as to whether God ever did place them there; and my belief is that we should be very slow to help back to the pulpit men who, having been tried once, have proved themselves to have too little grace to stand the crucial test of ministerial life.

For some work we choose none but the strong; and when God calls us to ministerial labour we should endeavour to get grace that we may be strengthened into fitness for our position, and not be mere novices carried away by the temptations of Satan, to the injury of the church and our own ruin. We are to stand equipped with the whole armour of God, ready for feats of valour not expected of others; to us self-denial, self-forgetfulness, patience, perseverance, longsuffering, must be everyday virtues, and who is sufficient for these things? We need to live very near to God if we want to approve ourselves in our vocation.

Recollect, as ministers, that your whole life, your whole pastoral life especially, will be affected by the vigour of your piety. If your zeal grows dull, you will not pray well in the pulpit; you will pray worse in the family, and worst in the study alone. When your soul becomes lean, your hearers, without knowing how or why, will find that your prayers in public have little savour for them; they will feel your barrenness, perhaps, before you perceive it yourself. Your discourses will next betray your declension. You may utter as well-chosen words, and as fitly-ordered sentences, as before; but there will be a perceptible loss of spiritual force. You will shake yourselves as at other times, even as Samson did, but you will find that your great strength has departed. In your daily communion with your people, they will not be slow to mark the all-pervading decline of your graces. Sharp eyes will see the grey hairs here and there long before you do. Let a man be afflicted with a disease of the heart, and all evils are wrapped up in that one – stomach, lungs, viscera, muscles, and nerves will all suffer; and so, let a man have his heart weakened in spiritual things, and very soon his entire life will feel the withering influence. Moreover, as the result of your own decline, everyone of your hearers will suffer more or less; the vigorous amongst them will overcome the depressing tendency, but the weaker sort will be seriously damaged. It is with us and our hearers as it is with watches and the public clock; if our watch is wrong, very few will be misled by it but ourselves; but if the Horse Guards or Greenwich Observatory should go wrong, half London would lose its reckoning. So it is with the minister; he is the parish clock, many take their time from him, and if he is incorrect, then they all go wrong, more or less, and he is in a great measure accountable for all the sin which he occasions. This we cannot endure to think of, my brethren. It will not bear a moment's comfortable consideration, and yet it must be looked at that we may guard against it.

Our danger is greater than that of others

On the whole, no place is so assailed with temptation as the ministry. Despite the popular idea that ours is a snug retreat from temptation, it is no less true that our dangers are more numerous and more insidious than those of ordinary Christians. Ours may be a vantage-ground for height, but that height is perilous, and to many the ministry has proved a Tarpeian rock.

If you ask what these temptations are, time might fail us to particularize them; but among them are both the coarse and the more refined; the coarse are such temptations as self-indulgence at the table, enticements to which are superabundant among a hospitable people, the temptations of the flesh, which are incessant with young unmarried men set on high among an admiring throng of your women: but enough of this, your own observation will soon reveal to you a thousand snares, unless indeed your eyes are blinded. There are more secret snares than these, from which we can less easily escape; and of these the worst is the temptation to ministerialism – the tendency to read our Bible as ministers, to pray as ministers, to get into doing the whole of our religion as not ourselves personally, but only relatively, concerned in it. To lose the personality of repentance and faith is a loss indeed. 'No man', says John Owen, 'preaches his sermon well to others if he doeth not first preach it to his own heart.' Brethren, it is eminently hard to keep to this. Our office, instead of helping our piety, as some assert, is through the evil of our natures turned into one of its most serious hindrances; at least, I find it so. How one kicks and struggles against officialism, and yet how easily does it beset us, like a long garment which twists around the racer's feet and impedes his running! Beware, dear brethren, of this and all the other seductions of your calling; and if you have done so until now, continue still to watch till life's latest hour.

We have noted but one of the perils, but indeed they are legion. The great enemy of souls takes care to leave no stone unturned for the preacher's ruin. Baxter says:

Take heed to yourselves, says Baxter, because the tempter will make his first and sharpest onset upon you. If you will be the leaders against him, he will spare you no further than God restraineth him. He breathe you the greatest malice that are engaged to do him the greatest mischief. As he hateth Christ more than any of us, because he is the General of the field, and the 'Captain of our salvation', and doth more than all the world besides against the kingdom of darkness; so doth he note the leaders under him more than the common soldiers, on the like account, in their proportion. He knows that a rout he may make among the rest, if the leaders fall before their eyes. He hath long tried that way of fighting, 'neither with small nor great,' comparatively, but these; and of 'smiting the shepherds, that he may scatter the flock.' And so great has been his success this way, that he will follow it on as far as he is able. Take heed, therefore, brethren, for the enemy hath a special eye upon you. You shall have his most subtle insinuations, and incessant solicitations, and violent assaults. As wise and learned as you are, take heed to yourselves lest he overwit you. The devil is a greater scholar than you are, and a nimbler disputant; he can 'transform himself into an angel of light' to deceive. He will get within you and trip up your heels before you are aware; he will play the juggler with you undiscerned, and cheat you of your faith or innocency, and you shall not know that you have lost it; nay, he will make you believe it is multiplied or increased when it is lost. You shall see neither hook nor line, much less the subtle angler himself, while he is offering you his bait. And his baits shall be so fitted to your temper and disposition, that he will be sure to find advantages within you, and make your own principles and inclinations to betray you; and whenever he ruineth you, he will make you the instrument of your own ruin. Oh, what a conquest will he think he hath got, if he can make a minister lazy and unfaithful; if he can tempt a minister into covetousness or scandal! He will glory against the church, and say, 'These are your holy preachers; you see what their preciseness is, and whither it will bring them.' He will glory against Jesus Christ himself, and say, 'These are thy champions! I can make thy chiefest servants to abuse thee; I can make the stewards of thy house unfaithful.' If he did so insult against God upon a false surmise, and tell him he could make Job to curse him to his face (Job 1:2), what would he do if he should indeed prevail

113

against us? And at last he will insult as much over you that ever he could draw you to be false to your great trust, and to blemish your holy profession, and to do him so much service that was your enemy. O do not so far gratify Satan; do not make him so much sport; suffer him not to use you as the Philistines did Samson – first to deprive you of your strength, and then to put out your eyes, and so to make you the matter of his triumph and derision.

Our work requires the highest degree of godliness

The labour of the Christian ministry is well performed in exact proportion to the vigour of our renewed nature. Our work is only well done when it is well with ourselves. As is the workman, such will the work be. To face the enemies of truth, to defend the bulwarks of the faith, to rule well in the house of God, to comfort all that mourn, to edify the saints, to guide the perplexed, to bear with the forward, to win and nurse souls – all these and a thousand other works beside are not for a Feeble-mind or a Ready-to-halt, but are reserved for Great-heart whom the Lord has made strong for himself. Seek then strength from the Strong One, wisdom from the Wise One, in fact, all from the God of all.

Our character must agree with our ministry

We have all heard the story of the man who preached so well and lived so badly that when he was in the pulpit everybody said he ought never to come out again, and when he was out of it they all declared he never ought to enter it again. May the Lord deliver us from the limitation of such a Janus. May we never be priests of God at the altar, and sons of Belial outside the tabernacle door; but on the contrary, may we, as Nazianzen says of Basil, 'thunder in our doctrine, and lighten in our conversation'. We do not trust those persons who have two faces, nor will men believe in those whose verbal and practical testimonies are contradictory. As actions, according to the proverb, speak louder than words, so an ill life will effectually drown the voice of the most eloquent ministry. After all, our truest building must be performed with our hands; our characters must be more persuasive than our speech. Here I would not alone warn you of sins of commission, but of sins of omission. Too many preachers forget to serve God when they are out of the pulpit, their lives are negatively inconsistent. Abhor, dear brethren, the thought of being clockwork ministers who are not alive by abiding grace within, but are wound up by temporary influences; men who are only ministers for the time being, under the stress of the hour of ministering, but cease to be ministers when they descend the pulpit stairs. True ministers are always ministers. Too many preachers are like those sand-toys we buy for our children: you turn the box upside down, and the little acrobat revolves and revolves till the sand is all run down, and then he hangs motionless; so there are some who persevere in the ministrations of truth as long as there is an official necessity for their work, but after that, no pay, no paternoster; no salary, no sermon.

It is a horrible thing to be an inconsistent minister. Our Lord is said to have been like Moses, for this reason, that he was 'a prophet mighty in word and in deed'. The man of God should imitate his Master in this; he should be mighty both in the word of his doctrine and in the deed of his example, and mightiest, if possible, in the second. It is remarkable that the only church history we have is *The Acts* of the Apostles'. The Holy Spirit has not preserved their sermons. They were very good ones, better than we shall ever preach, but still the Holy Spirit has only taken care of their 'acts'. We have no books of the resolutions of the apostles; when we hold our church meetings we record our minutes and resolutions, but the Holy Spirit only puts down the 'acts'. Our acts should be such as to bear recording, for recorded they will be. We must live as under the more immediate eye of God, and as in the blaze of the great all-revealing day.

What other authorities have said

Holiness in a minister is at once his chief necessity and his goodliest ornament. Mere moral excellence is not enough, there must be

115

the higher virtue, a consistent character there must be, but this must be anointed with the sacred consecrating oil, or that which makes us most fragrant to God and man will be wanting. Old John Stoughton, in his treatise *The Preacher's Dignity and Duty*, insists upon the minister's holiness in sentences full of weight.

> If Uzzah must die but for *touching the ark of God*, and that to stay it when it was like to fall; if the men of Beth-shemesh for *looking into it*; if the very beasts that do but come near the holy mount be threatened; then what manner of persons ought they to be who shall be admitted to talk with God familiarly, to 'stand before him,' as the angels do, and 'behold his face continually'; 'to bear his name before the Gentiles'; in a word, to be his ambassadors? 'Holiness becometh thy house, O Lord'; and were it not a ridiculous thing to imagine, that the vessels must be holy, but only he upon whose very garments must be written 'holiness to the Lord' might be unholy; that the bells of the horses should have an inscription of holiness upon them, in Zechariah, and the saints' bells, the bells of Aaron, should be unhallowed? No, they must be 'burning and shining lights', or else their influence will dart some malignant quality; they must 'chew the cud and divide the hoof', or else they are unclean; they must 'divide the word aright', and walk uprightly in their life, and so join life to learning. If holiness be wanting, the ambassadors dishonour the country from whence they come, and the prince from whom they come; and this dead Amasa, this dead doctrine not quickened with a good life, lying in the way, stops the people of the Lord, that they cannot go on cheerfully in their spiritual warfare.

The life of the preacher should be a magnet to draw men to Christ, and it is sad indeed when it keeps them from him. Sanctity in ministers is a loud call to sinners to repent, and when allied with holy cheerfulness it becomes wondrously attractive. Jeremy Taylor in his own rich language tells us:

116

Herod's doves could never have invited so many strangers to their dovecotes, if they had not been besmeared with opobalsamum; but, said Didymus, 'make your pigeons smell sweet, and they will allure whole flocks'; and if your life be excellent, if your virtues be like a precious ointment, you will soon invite your charges to run after your precious odours; but you must be excellent, a man of God, not after the common manner of men but 'after God's own heart'; and men will strive to be like you if you be like to God; but when you only stand at the door of virtue, for nothing but to keep sin out, you will draw into the folds of Christ none but such as glorify fear drives in. To do what will most glorify God, that is the line you must walk by; for to do no more than all men needs must is servility, not so much as the affection of sons; much less can you be fathers to the people, when you go not so far as the sons of God: for a dark lantern, though there be a weak brightness on one side, will scarce enlighten one, much less will it conduct a multitude, or allure many followers by the brightness of its flame.

Another equally admirable episcopal divine, Bishop Reynolds, has well and pithily said:

The star which led the wise men unto Christ, the pillar of fire which led the children unto Canaan, did not only shine, but go before them (Matthew 2:9; Exodus 13:21). The voice of Jacob will do little good if the hands be the hands of Esau. In the law, no person who had any blemish was to offer the oblations of the Lord (Leviticus 21:17-20); the Lord thereby teaching us what graces ought to be in his ministers. The priest was to have in his robes bells and pomegranates; the one of figure of sound doctrine, and the other of a fruitful life (Exodus 28:33-34). The Lord will be sanctified in all those that draw near unto him (Isaiah 52:11); for the sins of the priests make the people abhor the offering of the Lord (1 Samuel 2:17); their wicked lives do shame their doctrines;

117

as St Augustine says, with their doctrine they build, and with their lives they destroy. I conclude this point with that wholesome passage of Jerome: 'Let not thy works shame thy doctrine, lest they who hear thee in the church tacitly answer, Why doest thou not thyself what thou teachest to others?' He is too delicate a teacher who persuadeth others to fast with a full belly. A robber may accuse covetousness. A minister of Christ should have his tongue, and his heart, and his hand agree.

Very quaint also is the language of Thomas Playfere in his *Say Well, Do Well*:

There was a ridiculous actor in the city of Smyrna, who, pronouncing 'O heaven!', pointed with his finger towards the ground; which when Polemo, the chiefest man in the place, saw, he could abide to stay no longer, but went from the company in a great chafe, saying 'This fool hath made a solecism with his hand, he has spoken false Latin with his finger!' And such are they who *teach* well and *do* ill; that however they have *heaven* at their tongue's end, yet the *earth* is at their finger's end; such as do not only speak false Latin with their tongue, but false divinity with their hands; such as live not according to their preaching. But he that sits in the heaven will laugh them to scorn, and hiss them off the stage, if they do not mend their action.

The importance of little things

Even in little things the minister should take care that his life is consistent with his ministry. He should be especially careful never to fall short of his word. This should be pushed even to scrupulosity; we cannot be too careful; truth must not only be in us, but shine from us. A celebrated doctor of divinity in London, who is now in heaven I have no doubt – a very excellent and godly man – gave notice one Sunday that he intended to visit all his people, and said that in order to get round and visit them and their families once in the year, he would take all the seatholders in order. A person well known to me, who was then a poor man, was delighted with the idea that the minister was coming to his house to see him, and about a week or two before he conceived it would be his turn, his wife was very careful to sweep the hearth and keep the house tidy, and the man ran home early from work, hoping each night to find the doctor there. This went on for a considerable time. He either forgot his promise, or grew weary in performing it, or for some other reason never went to this poor man's house, and the result was this: the man lost all confidence in all preachers, and said, 'They care for the rich, but they do not care for us who are poor'. That man never settled down to any one place of worship for many years, till at last he dropped into Exeter Hall and remained my hearer for years till providence removed him. It was no small task to make him believe that any minister could be an honest man, and could impartially love both rich and poor. Let us avoid doing such mischief, by being very particular as to our word.

We must remember that we are very much looked at. Men hardly have the impudence to break the law in the open sight of their fellows, yet in such publicity we live and move. We are watched by a thousand eagle eyes; let us so act that we shall never need to care if all heaven, and earth, and hell, swelled the list of spectators. Our public position is a great gain if we are enabled to exhibit the fruits of the Spirit in our lives; take heed, brethren, that you do not throw away the advantage.

When we say to you, my dear brethren, take care of your life, we mean be careful of even the minutiae of your character. Avoid little debts, unpunctuality, gossiping, nicknaming, petty quarrels, and all other of those little vices which fill the ointment with flies. The self-indulgences which have lowered the repute of many must not be tolerated by us. The familiarities which have laid others under suspicion we must chastely avoid. The roughnesses which have rendered some obnoxious, and the fopperies which have made others contemptible, we must put away. We cannot afford to run great risks through little things. Our care must be to act on the rule, 'giving no offence in anything, that the ministry be not blamed'.

By this is not intended that we are to hold ourselves bound by every whim or fashion of the society in which we move. As a general rule, I hate the fashions of society, and detest conventionalities, and if I conceived it best to put my foot through a law of etiquette, I should feel gratified in having it to do. No, we are men, not slaves; and are not to relinquish our manly freedom, to be the lackeys of those who affect gentility or boast refinement. Yet, brethren, anything that verges on the coarseness which is akin to sin, we must shun as we would a viper. The rules of Chesterfield are ridiculous to us, but not the example of Christ; and he was never coarse, low, discourteous, or indelicate.

Even in your recreations, remember that you are ministers. When you are off the parade you are still officers in the army of Christ, and as such demean yourselves. But if the lesser things must be looked after, how careful should you be in the great matters of morality, honesty, and integrity! Here the minister must not fail. His private life must ever keep good tune with his ministry, or his day will soon set with him, and the sooner he retires the better, for his continuance in his office will only dishonour the cause of God and ruin himself.

The preacher's private prayer

Of course the preacher is distinguished above all others as a man of prayer. He prays as an ordinary Christian, or he would be a hypocrite. He prays more than ordinary Christians, or he would be disqualified for the office which he has undertaken. 'It would be wholly monstrous', says Bernard, 'for a man to be highest in office and lowest in soul; first in station and last in life.' Over all his other relationships the preeminence of the pastor's responsibility casts a halo, and if true to his Master, he becomes distinguished for his prayerfulness in them all. As a citizen, his country has the advantage of his intercession; as a neighbour those under his shadow are remembered in supplication. He prays as a husband and as a father; he strives to make his family devotions a model for his flock; and if the fire on the altar of God should burn low anywhere else, it is well tended in the house of the Lord's chosen servant – for he takes care that the morning and evening sacrifice shall sanctify his dwelling. But there are some of his prayers which concern his office. He offers special supplications *as a minister*, and he draws near to God in this respect over and above all his approaches in his other relationships.

A minister is always praying
Whenever his mind turns to his work, whether he is in it or out of it, the minister ejaculates a petition, sending up his holy desires as well-directed arrows to the skies. He is not always in the act of prayer, but he lives in the spirit of it. If his heart is in his work, he cannot eat or drink, or take recreation, or go to his bed, or rise in the morning, without evermore feeling a fervency of desire, a weight of anxiety, and a simplicity of dependence upon God; thus, in one form or other he continues in prayer. If there is any man under heaven who is compelled to carry out the precept 'Pray without ceasing', surely it is the Christian minister. He has peculiar temptations, special trials, singular difficulties, and remarkable duties, he has to deal with God in awful relationships, and with men in mysterious interests; he therefore needs much more grace than common men, and as he knows this, he is led constantly to cry to the strong for strength, and say, 'I will life up mine eyes unto the hills, from when cometh my help.' Alleine once wrote to a dear friend:

Though I am apt to be unsettled and quickly set off the hinges, yet, methinks, I am like a bird out of the nest, I am never quiet till I am in my old way of communion with God; like the needle in the compass, that is restless till it be turned towards the pole. I can say, through grace, with the church, 'With my soul have I desired thee in the night, and with my

121

spirit within me have I sought thee early.' My heart is early and late with God; 'tis the business and delight of my life to seek him.

Such must be the even tenor of your way, O men of God. If you ministers are not very prayerful, you are much to be pitied. If, in the future, you are called to sustain pastorates, large or small, if you become lax in secret devotion, not only will *you* need to be pitied, but your people also; and, in addition to that, you will be blamed, and the day will come when you will be ashamed and confounded.

The value of private prayer

It may scarcely but needful to commend to you the sweet uses of private devotion, and yet I cannot forbear. To you, as the ambassadors of God, the mercy-seat has a virtue beyond all estimate; the more familiar you are with the court of heaven the better you will discharge your heavenly trust. Among all the formative influences which go back to make up a man honoured by God in the ministry, I know of none more mighty than his own familiarity with the mercy-seat. All that a college course can do for a student is coarse and external compared with the spiritual and delicate refinement obtained by communion with God. While the unformed minister is revolving upon the wheel of preparation, prayer is the tool of the great plotter by which he moulds the vessel. All our libraries and studies are mere emptiness compared with our closets. We grow, we become mighty, we prevail in private prayer.

Your prayers will be your ablest assistants *while your discourses are still on the anvil*. While other men, like Esau, are hunting for their portion, you, by the aid of prayer, will find the savoury meat near at home, and may say in truth what Jacob said so falsely, 'The Lord brought it to me'. If you can dip your pens into your hearts, appealing in earnestness to the Lord, you will write well; and if you can gather your matter on your knees at the gate of heaven, you will not fail to speak well. Prayer, as a mental exercise, will bring many subjects before the mind, and so help in the selection of a topic, while as a high spiritual engagement it will cleanse your inner eye that you may see truth in the light of God. Texts will often refuse to reveal their treasures till you open them with the key of prayer. How wonderfully were the books opened to Daniel when he was in supplication! How much Peter learned upon the housetop! The closet is the best study. The commentators are good instructors, but the Author himself is far better, and prayer makes a direct appeal to him and enlists him in our cause. It is a great thing to pray oneself into the spirit and marrow of a text; working into it by sacred feeding on it, just as the worm bores its way into the kernel of the nut. Prayer supplies a leverage for the uplifting of ponderous truths. One marvels how the stones of Stonehenge could have been set in their places; it is even more to be inquired after where some men obtained such admirable knowledge of mysterious doctrines: was not prayer the potent machinery which wrought the wonder? Waiting on God often turns darkness into light. Persevering enquiry at the sacred oracle uplifts the veil and gives grace to look into the deep things of God.

A certain Puritan divine at a debate was observed frequently to write upon the paper before him; upon others curiously seeking to read his notes, they found nothing upon the page but the words, 'More light, Lord,' 'More light, Lord,' repeated scores of times: a most suitable prayer for the student of the Word when preparing his discourse.

You will frequently find fresh streams of thought leaping up from the passage before you, as if the rock had been struck by Moses' rod; new veins of precious ore will be revealed to your hammer of prayer. You will sometimes feel as if you were entirely shut up, and then suddenly a new road will open before you. He who has the key of David opens, and no one shuts. If you have ever sailed down the Rhine, the water scenery of that majestic river will have struck you as being very like in effect to a series of lakes. Before and behind the vessel appears to be enclosed in massive walls of rock, or circles of vine-clad terraces, till on a sudden you turn a corner, and before you the rejoicing and abounding river flows onward in its strength. So the laborious student often finds it with a text; it appears to be fast closed against you, but prayer propels your vessel, and turns its prow into fresh waters, and you behold the broad and deep stream of sacred truth flowing in its fullness, and bearing you with it. Is not this a convincing reason for abiding in supplication? Use prayer as a boring rod, and wells of living water will leap up from the bowels of the Word. Who will be content to thirst when living waters are so readily to be obtained?

Prayer and preaching
Preparing the sermon
The best and holiest men have always made prayer the most important part of pulpit preparation. It is said of M'Cheyne:

> Anxious to give his people on the Sabbath what had cost him somewhat, he never, without an urgent reason, went before them without much previous meditation and prayer. His principle on this subject was embodied in a remark he made to some of us who were conversing on the matter. Being asked his view of diligent preparation for the pulpit, he reminded us of Exodus 27:20: *'Beaten oil – beaten oil for the lamps of the sanctuary.'* And yet his prayerfulness was greater still. Indeed, he could not neglect fellowship with God before entering the congregation. He needed to be bathed in the love of God. His ministry was so much a bringing out of views that had first sanctified his own soul, that the healthiness of his soul was absolutely needful to the vigour and power of his ministrations. . . With him the commencement of all labour invariably consisted in the preparation of his own soul. The walls of his chamber were witnesses of his prayerfulness and of his tears, as well as of his cries.

Delivering the sermon
Prayer will singularly assist you in the delivery of your sermon; in fact, nothing can so gloriously fit you to preach as descending fresh from

the mount of communion with God to speak with men. None are so able to plead with men as those who have been wrestling with God on their behalf. It is said of Alleine, 'He poured out his very heart in prayer and preaching. His supplications and his exhortations were so affectionate, so full of holy zeal, life and vigour, that they quite overcame his hearers; he melted over them, so that he thawed and mollified, and sometimes dissolved the hardest hearts.' There could have been none of this sacred dissolving of heart if his mind had not been previously exposed to the tropical rays of the Sun of Righteousness by private fellowship with the risen Lord. A truly moving delivery, in which there is no affectation, but much affection, can only be the offspring of prayer. There is no rhetoric like that of the heart, and no school for learning it but the foot of the cross. It were better that you never learned a rule of human oratory, but were full of the power of heavenborn love, than that you should master Quintilian, Cicero, and Aristotle, and remain without the apostolic anointing.

Prayer may not make you eloquent after the human mode, but it will make you truly so, for you will speak out of the heart; and is not that the meaning of the word eloquence? It will bring fire from heaven upon your sacrifice, and thus prove it to be accepted of the Lord.

As fresh springs of thought will frequently break up during preparation in answer to prayer, so will it be in the delivery of the sermon. Most preachers who depend upon God's Spirit will tell you that their freshest and best thoughts are not those which were premeditated, but ideas which come to them, flying as on the wings of angels; unexpected treasures brought on a sudden by celestial hands, seeds of the flowers of paradise, wafted from the mountains of myrrh. Often and often when I have felt hampered, both in thought and expression, my secret groaning of heart has brought me relief, and I have enjoyed more than usual liberty. But how dare we pray in the battle if we have never cried to the Lord while buckling on the harness? The remembrance of his wrestlings at home comforts the fettered preacher when in the pulpit: God will not desert us unless we have deserted him. You, brethren, will find that prayer will ensure you strength equal to your day.

As the tongues of fire came upon the apostles, when they sat watching and praying, even so will they come upon you. You will find yourselves, when you might perhaps have flagged, suddenly borne up as by a seraph's power. Wheels of fire will be fastened to your chariot, which had begun to drag right heavily, and steeds angelic will be in a moment harnessed to your fiery car, till you climb the heavens like Elijah, in a rapture of flaming inspiration.

After the sermon

How would a conscientious preacher give vent to his feelings and find solace for his soul if access to the mercy-seat were denied him? Elevated to the highest pitch of excitement, how can we relive our souls but in importunate pleadings? Or, depressed by a fear of failure, how shall we be comforted but in moaning out our complaint before our God? How often have some of us tossed to and fro upon our couch half the night because of conscious short-comings in our testimony! How frequently have we longed to rush back to the pulpit again to say over again more vehemently what we have uttered in so cold a manner! Where could we find rest for our spirits but in confession of sin, and passionate entreaty that our folly might in no way hinder the Spirit of God!

It is not possible in a public assembly to pour out all our heart's love to our flock. Like Joseph, the affectionate minister will seek somewhere to weep; his emotions, however freely he may express himself, will be pent up in the pulpit, and only in private prayer can he draw up the sluices and bid them flow forth. If we cannot prevail with men for God, we will, at least, endeavour to prevail with God for men. We cannot save them, or even persuade them to be saved, but we can at least bewail their madness and entreat the interference of the Lord. Like Jeremiah, we can make it our resolve, 'If ye will not hear it, my soul shall weep in secret places for your pride, and mine eye shall weep sore and run down with tears'. The Lord's heart can never be indifferent to such moving appeals; in due time

126

the weeping intercessor will become the rejoicing winner of souls.

There is a distinct connection between importunate agonizing and true success, just as there is between the travail and the birth, the sowing in tears and the reaping in joy. 'How is it that your seed comes up so soon?' said one gardener to another. 'Because I steep it,' was the reply. We must steep all our teachings in tears, 'when none but God is nigh', and their growth will surprise and delight us.

The secret of preachers' success

Could anyone wonder at Brainerd's success, when his diary contains such notes as this:

> Lord's Day, April 25th – This morning spent about two hours in sacred duties, and was enabled, more than ordinarily, to agonize for immortal souls; though it was early in the morning, and the sun scarcely shone at all, yet my body was quite wet with sweat.

The secret of Luther's power lay in the same direction. Theodorus said of him: 'I overheard him in prayer, but, good God, with what life and spirit did he pray! It was with so much reverence, as if he were speaking to God, yet with so much confidence as if he were speaking to his friend.'

My brethren, let me beseech you to be men of prayer. Great talents you may never have, but you will do well enough without them if you abound in intercession. If you do not pray over what you have sown, God's sovereignty may possibly determine to give a blessing, but you have no right to expect it, and if it comes it will bring no comfort to your own heart.

I was reading yesterday a book by Father Faber, late of the Oratory, at Brompton, a marvellous compound of truth and error. In it he relates a legend to this effect. A certain preacher, whose sermons converted men by scores, received a revelation from heaven that not one of the conversions was owing to his talents or eloquence, but all to the prayers of an illiterate lay-brother, who sat on the pulpit steps, pleading all the time for the success of the sermon. It may in the all-revealing day be so with us. We may discover, after having laboured long and wearily in preaching, that all the honour belongs to another builder, whose prayers were gold, silver, and precious stones, while our sermonizings being apart from prayer, were but hay and stubble.

Intercession

When we have done with preaching, we shall not, if we are true ministers of God, have done with praying, because the whole church, with many tongues, will be crying, in the language of the Macedonian, 'Come over and help us' in prayer. If you are enabled to prevail in prayer you will have many requests to offer for others who will flock to you, and beg a share in our intercessions, and so you will find yourselves commissioned with errands to the mercy-seat for friends and hearers. Such is always my lot, and I feel it a pleasure to have such requests to present before my Lord. Never can you be short of themes for prayer, even if no one should suggest them to you. Look at your congregation. There are always sick folk among them, and many more who are soul-sick. Some are unsaved, others are seeking and cannot find. Many are desponding, and not a few believers are backsliding or mourning. There are widows' tears and orphans' sighs to be put into our bottle, and poured out before the Lord. If you are a genuine minister of God you will stand as a priest before the Lord, spiritually wearing the ephod and the breastplate whereon you bear the names of the children of Israel, pleading for them within the veil. I have known brethren who have kept a list of persons for whom they felt bound especially to pray, and I doubt not such a record often reminded them of what might otherwise have slipped their memory. Nor will your people wholly engross you; the nation and the world will claim their share. The man who is mighty in prayer may be a wall of fire around his country, her guardian angel and her shield. We have all heard how the enemies of the Protestant cause dreaded the prayers of Knox more than they feared armies of ten thousand men. The famous Welch was also a great intercessor for his country; he used to say he wondered how a Christian could lie in his bed all night and not rise to pray. When his wife, fearing that he would catch cold, followed him into the room to which he had withdrawn, she heard him pleading in broken sentences, 'Lord, wilt thou not grant me Scotland?' Of that we were thus wrestling at midnight, crying, 'Lord, wilt thou not grant us our hearers' souls?'

The minister who does not earnestly pray over his work must surely be a vain and conceited man. He acts as if he thought himself sufficient of himself, and therefore did not need to appeal to God. Yet what a baseless pride to conceive that our preaching can ever be in itself so powerful that it can turn men from their sins, and bring them to God without the working of the Holy Spirit. If we are truly humble-minded we shall not venture down to the fight until the Lord of Hosts has clothed us with all power, and said to us, 'Go in this thy might'. The preacher who neglects to pray much must be very careless about his ministry. He cannot have comprehended his calling. He cannot have computed the value of a soul, or estimated the meaning of eternity. He must be a mere official, tempted into a pulpit because the piece of bread which belongs to the priest's office is very necessary to him, or a detestable hypocrite who loves the praise of men, and cares not for the praise of God. He will surely become a mere superficial talker, best approved where grace is least valued and a vain show most admired. He cannot be one of those who plough deep and reap abundant harvests. He is a mere loiterer, not a labourer. As a preacher he has a name to live and is dead. He limps in his life like the lame man in the Proverbs, whose legs were not equal, for his prayer is shorter than his preaching.

I am afraid that, more or less, most of us need self-examination as to this matter. If any man here should venture to say that he prays as much as he ought, as a student, I should gravely question his statement; and if there is a minister, deacon, or elder present who can say that he believes he is occupied with God in prayer to the full extent to which he might be, I should be pleased to know him. I can only say that if he can claim this excellence, he leaves me far behind, for I can make no such claim. I wish I could; and I make the confession with no small degree of shamefacedness and confusion, but I am obliged to make it. If we are not more negligent than others, this is no consolation to us; the shortcomings of others are no excuses for us.

Great men of prayer

How few of us could compare ourselves with Mr Joseph Alleine, whose character I have mentioned before? His wife writes:

> At the time of his health, he did rise constantly at or before four of the clock, and would be much troubled if he heard smiths or other craftsmen at their trades before he was at communion with God; saying to me often, 'How this noise shames me. Does not my Master deserve more than theirs?' From four till eight he spent in prayer, holy contemplation, and singing of psalms, in which he much delighted and did daily practise alone, as well as in the family. Sometimes he would suspend the routine of parochial engagements, and devote whole days to these secret exercises, in order to which, he would contrive to be alone in some void house, or else in some sequestered spot in the open valley. Here there would be much prayer and meditation on God and heaven.

Could we read Jonathan Edwards' description of David Brainerd and not blush?

> His life shows the right way to success in the works of the ministry. He sought it as a resolute soldier seeks victory in a siege or battle; or as a man that runs a race for a great price. Animated with love to Christ and souls, how did he labour always fervently, not only in word and doctrine, in public and private, but in *prayers* day and night, 'wrestling with God' in secret, and 'travailing in birth', with unutterable groans and

130

agonies, 'until Christ was formed' in the hearts of the people to whom he was sent! How did he thirst for a blessing upon his ministry, 'and watch for souls as one that must give account'! How did he go forth in the strength of the Lord God, seeking and depending on the special influence of the Spirit to assist and succeed him! And what was the happy fruit at last, after long waiting and many dark and discouraging appearances; like a true son of Jacob, he persevered in wrestling through all the darkness of the night, until the breaking of the day.

Might not Henry Martyn's journal shame us, where we find such entries as these:

September 24th – The determination with which I went to bed last night, of devoting this day to prayer and fasting, I was enabled to put into execution. In my first prayer for deliverance from worldly thoughts, depending on the power and promises of God, for fixing my soul while I prayed, I was helped to enjoy much abstinence from the world for nearly an hour. Then read the history of Abraham, to see how familiarly God had revealed himself to mortal men of old. Afterwards, in prayer for my own sanctification, my soul breathed freely and ardently after the holiness of God, and this was the best season of the day.

We might perhaps more truly join with him in his lament after the first year of his ministry that he judged he had dedicated too much time to public ministrations, and too little to private communion with God.

How much of blessing we may have missed through remissness in supplication we can scarcely guess, and none of us can know how poor we are in comparison with what we might have been if we had lived habitually nearer to God in prayer. Vain regrets and surmises are useless, but an earnest determination to amend will be far more useful. We not only ought to pray more, but we *must*. The fact is, the secret of all ministerial success lies in prevalence at the mercy-seat.

Unction from above

One bright benison which private prayer brings down upon the ministry is an indescribable and inimitable something, better understood than named; it is a dew from the Lord, a divine presence which you will recognize at once when I say it is 'an unction from the holy One'. What is it? I wonder how long we might beat our brains before we could plainly put into words what is meant by *preaching with unction*; yet he who preaches knows its presence, and he who hears soon detects its absence; Samaria, in famine, typifies a discourse without it; Jerusalem, with her feasts of fat things full of marrow, may represent a sermon enriched with it.

Counterfeit signs

Everyone knows what the freshness of the morning is when orient pearls abound on every blade of grass, but who can describe it, much less produce it of itself? Such is the mystery of spiritual anointing; we know, but we cannot tell to others what it is. It is as easy as it is foolish to counterfeit it, as some do who use expressions which are meant to betoken fervent love, but oftener indicate sickly sentimentalism of mere cant. 'Dear Lord!' 'Sweet Jesus!' 'Precious Christ!' are by them poured out wholesale, till one is nauseated. These familiarities may have been not only tolerable, but even beautiful when they first fell from a saint of God, speaking, as it were, out of the excellent glory, but when repeated flippantly they are not only intolerable, but indecent, if not profane.

Some have tried to imitate unction by unnatural tones and whines; by turning up the whites of their eyes, and lifting their hands in a most ridiculous manner. M'Cheyne's tone and rhythm one hears from Scotchmen continually: we much prefer his spirit to his mannerism; and all mere mannerism without power is as foul carrion bereft of all life, obnoxious, mischievous.

Certain brethren aim at inspiration through exertion and loud shouting, but it does not come; some we have known to stop the

132

discourse, and exclaim 'God bless you', and others gesticulate wildly, and drive their fingernails into the palms of their hands as if they were in convulsions of celestial ardour. Bah! The whole thing smells of the green-room and the stage. The getting up of fervour in hearers by the simulation of it in the preacher is a loathsome deceit to be scorned by honest men. 'To affect feeling', says Richard Cecil, 'is nauseous and soon detected, but to feel is the readiest way to the hearts of others.' Unction is a thing which you cannot manufacture, and its counterfeits are worse than worthless; yet it is in itself priceless, and beyond measure needful if you would edify believers and bring sinners to Jesus. To the secret pleader with God this secret is committed; upon him rests the dew of the Lord, about him is the perfume which makes the heart glad. If the anointing which we bear does not come from the Lord of hosts we are deceivers, and since only in prayer can we obtain it, let us continue instant, constant, fervent in supplication. Let your fleece lie on the threshing-floor of supplication till it is wet with the dew of heaven. Do not go to minister in the temple till you have washed in the laver. Do not think to be a messenger of grace to others till you have seen the God of grace for yourselves, and had the Word from his mouth.

Times of quiet

Time spent in quiet prostration of soul before the Lord is most invigorating. David sat before the Lord; it is a great thing to hold these sacred sittings; the mind being receptive, like an open flower drinking in the sunbeams, or the sensitive photographic plate accepting the image before it. Quietude, which some men cannot abide, because it reveals their inward poverty, is as a palace of cedar to the wise, for along its hallowed courts the King in his beauty deigns to walk.

> Sacred silence! thou that art
> Floodgate of the deeper heart,
> Offspring of a heavenly kind;
> Frost o' the mouth, and thaw o' the mind.
>
> (Flecknoe)

Priceless as the gift of utterance may be, the practice of silence in some aspects far excels it. Do you think me a Quaker? Well, be it so. In this I follow George Fox most lovingly; for I am persuaded that we most of us think too much of speech, which after all is but the shell of thought. Quiet contemplation, still worship, unuttered rapture, these are mine when my best jewels are before me. Brethren, do not rob your heart of the deep sea joys; do not miss the far-down life, by for ever babbling among the broken shells and foaming surges of the shore.

Special times of prayer

I would seriously recommend to you, when settled in the ministry, the celebration of extraordinary sessions of devotion. If your ordinary prayers do not keep up the freshness and vigour of your souls, and you feel that you are flagging, get alone for a week, or even a month if possible. We have occasional holidays, why not frequent holy days? We hear of our richer brethren finding time for a journey to Jerusalem; could we not spare time for the less difficult and far more profitable journey to the heavenly city? Isaac Ambrose, once pastor at Preston, who wrote that famous book *Looking unto Jesus*, always set apart one month in the year for seclusion in a hut in a wood at Garstang. No wonder that he was so mighty a divine, when he could regularly spend so long a time in the mount with God. I notice that the Roman Catholics are accustomed to secure what they call 'retreats', where a number of priests will retire for a time into perfect quietude, to spend the whole of the time in fasting and prayer, so as to inflame their souls with ardour. We may learn from our adversaries. It would be a great thing every now and then for a band of truly spiritual brethren to spend a day or two with each other in real burning agony of prayer. Pastors alone could use much more freedom than in a mixed company. Times of humiliation and supplication for the whole church will also benefit us if we enter into them heartily. Our seasons of fasting and prayer at the Tabernacle have been high days indeed; never has heaven's gate stood wider; never have our hearts

134

been nearer the central glory. I look forward to our month of special devotion, as mariners reckon upon reaching land. Even if our public work were laid aside to give us space for special prayer, it might be a great gain to our churches. A voyage to the golden rivers of fellowship and meditation would be well repaid by a freight of sanctified feeling and elevated thought. Our silence might be better than our voices if our solitude were went with God. That was a grand action of old Jerome, when he laid all his pressing engagements aside to achieve a purpose to which he felt a call from heaven. He had a large congregation, as large a one as any of us need want; but he said to his people, 'Now it is of necessity that the New Testament should be translated, you must find another preacher: the translation must be made; I am bound for the wilderness, and shall not return till my task is finished.' Away he went with his manuscripts, and prayed and laboured, and produced a work – the Latin Vulgate – which will last as long as the world stands; on the whole a most wonderful translation of Holy Scripture. As learning and prayerful retirement together could thus produce an immortal work, if we were sometimes to say to our people when we felt moved to do so, 'Dear friends, we really must be gone for a little while to refresh our souls in solitude,' our profiting would soon be apparent, and if we did not write Latin Vulgates, yet we should do immortal work, such as would abide the fire.

Spurgeon's letters

Pastoral letters

In the early years of his ministry, it was Mr Spurgeon's custom to write an annual letter to his people. This series of pastoral letters, from 1857 to 1862, gives a bird's-eye view of the progress of the work from the memorable night of the great catastrophe in the Music Hall to the happy settlement of the congregation in the Metropolitan Tabernacle. All of the letters show the Pastor's intense desire for the growth in grace of the brothers and sisters in fellowship with the church, and for the ingathering of those who were still 'out of the way'.

1857
Dearly beloved,
We have hitherto been assisted by our Covenant Head; let us praise and thank him. Dark have been some of the dealings of providence towards us; but however such we may lament, we cannot alter; let us therefore give our time to action rather than regret.

Our numbers have been multiplied, and our zeal maintained; for this let us be grateful. And now that we enter upon another period of time, what shall we do in it? Let our answer be that, through God's grace, we will be devoted to his cause, and seek out means of glorifying him. Our hearts are set upon A LARGER TABER-NACLE. Will we not labour to immortalize this year by laying the foundation stone thereof? I am persuaded that God demands it; will we not delight to give him all his cause requires?

The Lord has been on our side, and through much opposition he has preserved us unscathed. Let us build him a house to his honour, which will be the means of making known his glory, and discomfiting his enemies.

The church of Christ will help us; but, if all forsake us, by God's help let us do it alone. We have hitherto had the answer to that prayer of Moses, 'Let his hands be sufficient for him'; and it shall not fail us now. We will toil together with one warm heart until the topstone be laid, and then our prayer shall be, 'Lord, fill the house with thy glory!'

May every blessing attend you in your families, in our businesses, and especially in your souls; and may pastor and people meet in glory!

'Trust in the Lord, and do good.'

1858

Dearly beloved,

We again acknowledge the goodness of our Covenant Lord. Last year, we wrote in faith. Surrounded by dark clouds, we believed that all things would work for our good; and now, rejoicing in hope, we record the fulfilment of the promise. The huge waves which Satan stirred against us have not caused us damage; but, by God's good grace, we have surmounted every billow, and are still sailing on to our desired haven. This has been the greatest year of all. Every Sabbath, crowds have filled the Music Hall; and every month, the pool of baptism has witnessed that they have not heard in vain.

Let us be grateful for past indulgence, and let us be on the look-out for trial. We must not expect to be let alone. Satan has many plots; and though signally foiled in one, another may be ready. Be prayerful, that trial come not upon us as a thief in the night; be

137

watchful, lest we ourselves should, by our sloth, become the instruments of our own ruin.

The Tabernacle Fund progresses beyond our hopes. It is most probable that, before the end of the year, we shall have far exceeded £5000, which is no small sum. Another year of earnest effort, and the work will be nearing a conclusion. 'Bless the Lord, O my soul; and all that is within me, bless his holy name.' The Lord will prosper that which concerneth us; we shall continue in loving labour, knit together as the heart of one man; and, by-and-by, we shall raise the topstone to its place amidst the shouts of the people.

I am anxious beyond measure for your purity and unity. I pray you, watch over one another in the Lord, and may the Master himself keep us all by his grace! Accept your minister's most hearty love, with every good wish for yourselves and your families; and be not unmindful to offer fervent prayer for our success and preservation. Your minister's motto is – 'ON! ON! ON!' Let yours be – 'GO FORWARD'.

1859

Dearly beloved and longed for, my joy and crown,
May the blessing of the Most High God descend upon you in answer to my earnest prayers! This has been a year of prayer. I thank God for the daily supplications which you have presented at the throne of grace. Rest assured that your pastor appreciates your affectionate earnestness on his behalf, and is greatly strengthened and encouraged thereby. It often brings tears of joy to my eyes when, in the midst of weary labour and cruel abuse, I remember your united prayers. May God hear you, and make me a better preacher, causing my labours among you to be more successful, both in your edification and increase!

Permit me to counsel you as to the training of your families. I would have all our children fully taught the Word of God. Let me strongly recommend to you the use of *The Assembly's Catechism*. Many a minister has derived his first doctrinal knowledge from that book; and, indeed, it has in it the very lifeblood of the Gospel. Let our youths and maidens study the scriptures daily, and let them use *The Baptist Confession of Faith*, which they will find to be a useful compendium of doctrinal knowledge. My desire is that I may have around me a well-instructed people, who shall be able to give a reason for the hope which is in them.

There are many among us who are, at present, cold or lukewarm; may the divine fire which is in some of you be kindled in their hearts also! Cleave to the Lord with purpose of heart, and the fellowship of the Holy Spirit be with you!

1860

My very dear friends,

I am glad of this opportunity to assure you of the continuance and increase of my hearty and undissembled love to you. Each year unites us more firmly. We have suffered together, and we have also rejoiced together. In the cause of our common Master, we have alike endured the reproach of men, and the reviling of the people; and in the success which has attended us, we have had to rejoice in the smile of a Covenant God, and in the energy of his Spirit. Comrades in battle, we are also co-heirs of victory. May the Lord, whom I serve in the Gospel of his Son, abundantly bless you, and return into your bosoms a thousandfold those acts of love, and those words of affection, by which you so perpetually prove your earnest attachment to me! Never had a pastor a better flock; never did a minister more sincerely long for the good of his people. And now, brethren, suffer the word of exhortation which I address to you:

In relation to myself

I beseech you, cease not to plead with God on my behalf. I have always acknowledged and recognized the value of the supplications of my church, and I feel the necessity of your earnest prayers more than ever. I entreat you, as the spiritual father of very many of you, cease not to intercede with God on my behalf.

In relation to the deacons and elders

Let me indulge the hope that our church shall become as scriptural in its order as in its doctrines; and let me go further, let me hope that we may not only walk in scriptural order, but in spiritual power. Seek unitedly the purity and increase of the whole body. Rally round the officers of our little army, and submit yourselves to their guidance and counsel. Let every member know the elder who presides over his district; and should that brother fail to visit him, let the member visit the elder, and remind him that he has overlooked one of the sheep of his flock. Endeavour to maintain meetings for prayer in each district of this great city; and if there be a door for other agencies, use them to the utmost of your ability. Each district, with its elder, should be a regiment with its officer; and then all the different bands, when called to united action, would be ready to achieve an easy victory. Honour the brethren who serve you in the Gospel, and esteem them very highly in love, for the Lord's sake.

In relation to one another

I admire the liberality of our poor brethren to the cause, and the zeal of all for the spread of the truth, and the love which exists among you one toward another. 'Let brotherly love continue.' We are none of us perfect, and therefore need forbearance from others; our fellow-members are like, ourselves, and therefore we must exercise the like charity towards them. We must mutually seek the comfort and sanctification of each other, 'endeavouring to keep the unity of the Spirit in the bond of peace'.

A meek and quiet temper will always tend to sustain you under injuries from others, and will prevent your dealing harshly with brethren. The character of Archbishop Leighton is one which it would be a noble thing for us to imitate to the letter. Speaking of his humility, Burnet says that 'he seemed to have the lowest thoughts of himself possible, and to desire that all other persons should think as meanly of him as he did of himself; and he bore all sorts of ill-usage and reproach, like a man that took pleasure in it.' And again, of his temperament, 'he had so subdued the natural heat of his temper that, in a great variety of circumstances, and in the course of intimate conversation with him for twenty years, he never observed the least sign of passion in him, but upon one occasion.' The accidents and behaviour which usually disturb the temper had no power to ruffle the equanimity of Leighton. Whilst living at Dunblane, his manservant, being desirous of fishing, went off one morning very early, locking the door, and taking the key with him, thus making his master a prisoner; nor did he return until the evening, when the only rebuke which he received from the Bishop was, 'John, when you next go a-fishing, remember to leave the key in the door.' Perhaps it is too much to expect so great a degree of gracious temper in all; but, nevertheless, let us strive after it. This will make it easy work to maintain cordial and joyous communion.

In relation to other churches
Be careful to maintain your orthodoxy, and bear your witness against all error; but be even more mindful to secure the communion of saints, and avoid all bigotry and bitterness.

With regard to the world
Let it not seduce you; come out from it daily, and be separate; but strive daily for the salvation of souls; and may the Lord make you, in his hands, the salt of the earth, and the instructors of the people! Huge is our city, and hideous its sin; labour for the good of men, and finally, when the chief Shepherd shall appear, may we all appear with him in glory!

1861
Brothers and Sisters,

Bless God for the past, and trust him for the future. It is far better to prepare for what lies before us than to congratulate ourselves upon that which is already accomplished. Great as have been the blessings with which almighty God has favoured us, we are longing and looking for larger displays of his goodness. Permit me very lovingly to thank you all for your hearty assistance in labours already performed, and allow me to entreat your continued aid in our new undertakings. Above all things, I most earnestly crave your prayers; and I am sure you will not deny them to me.

Pray for me in my ministry

It is no narrow sphere to which my Lord has called me. Nothing but all-sufficient grace can enable me to discharge the labours which devolve upon me. Oh, I beseech you, as Aarons and Hurs, hold up my hands, that my pulpit power may not abate!

Pray for me as pastor

The church is of so great a magnitude that no eye but that of Omniscience can oversee it all. As a company of fallible men, we have many infirmities; and it is a matchless favour to deal faithfully with all, and yet maintain perfect peace; to be ever active in stirring up the whole company, and yet very tender and pitiful to the lambs of the flock. Pray for me, my beloved, for I would rather renounce my office than lack your prayers.

Pray for me as an evangelist

I am incessantly itinerating through the cities, towns, and villages of this land. There are few large towns in which I have not uplifted the cross of Christ. These frequent journeyings require much physical strength; and constant preaching demands great mental power, and spiritual might. Ask of my Lord that, everywhere, his Word may have free course, run, and be glorified. There are lifeless churches to be aroused, and careless sinners to be called. Entreat our heavenly Father that my preaching may have a share of success in promoting these most important objects.

Pray for me as a teacher of teachers

The Lord put it into my heart to commence an institution for the training of young ministers. With a very able coadjutor, I have constantly increased the number of young men. Prayer and faith have always supplied the means so far, although I have no society or regular funds to depend upon. I would rejoice greatly if my gracious Lord would send me pecuniary aid to enable me to increase the number at once to twenty. This I must leave with him. Much wisdom is needed in training uncultivated but earnest minds, and in finding suitable sphere for the men when they are ready for the work. Let this matter, then, be remembered at the mercy-seat so often as it shall be well with you.

Pray for me as an intercessor for others
Beg that the Lord may give me power in prayer. The most of a minister's work must be done upon his knees. Weak here, we are weak everywhere. I desire to bear you ever on my heart before the throne; but how can I do this unless you shall pray the Lord to enable me? For this, I appeal to you, and beg your perpetual remembrances.

Finally, brethren, wait for the appearance of the Lord from heaven, and be ye found with well-trimmed lamps and well-girt loins, that, when he comes, you may rejoice before him.

1862
To the Church in the Metropolitan Tabernacle, over which the Lord has made me overseer.
Beloved Friends,
Your faithfulness and affection are gratefully remembered in my daily thanksgivings and in this public manner I tender you my warmest gratitude. Truly, I have no cause to complain of fickle or lukewarm friends in the church. No abuse, however venomous, has shaken your confidence; no misrepresentations, however scurrilous, have loosened your attachment. We have borne equally and cheerfully the cross of Christ. You have not repudiated the burden, as though it belonged only to the pastor; but you have felt that an attack upon him was an assault upon yourselves, and any wounds which he might suffer have rankled in your spirit as well as in his own. Persecution has been greatly blessed to us, for it has made us a united people; and we may add, a separated company, who are constantly constrained to contend for one another against the

world, both religious and profane. A thousand times have the haters of our holy cause uttered the most villainous calumnies against your pastor; but, as one by one you have heard their report, they have no more alarmed you than the crackling of thorns in the fire, or the noise of summer insects among the trees. We can afford to endure this 'trial of cruel mockings', for a clear conscience, prevalence in prayer, and abundant success are an armour quite sufficient for the church in her worst condition.

During the past year, we have entered upon our new Tabernacle, having no debt to encumber our future action. What a cause for gratitude to our all-gracious, prayer-hearing God! And what a claim upon us to exercise abundant faith and entire consecration to his cause! The Lord has not dealt thus with every people; let us be glad and rejoice in him.

Since the opening of the building, very many necessary works have been performed which have engrossed the larger part of the annual revenue; and much remains still to be done before the Tabernacle can be called complete; hence there will be little or nothing to spare for the College, and the pastor must look to your thank-offerings for the support of this great cause. You have not been backward aforetime, and will certainly be ready now.

With regard to our spiritual interests, let us ask ourselves whether we have grown in grace this year, whether, like the living tree, we have put forth fresh branches and leaves, or whether we have stood like posts, on which the rain descends and the dew distils, but they remain as dead and unfruitful as before. Is our faith stronger? Is our love warmer? Is our hope brighter? Have we advanced in courage, patience, virtue, and true holiness? Has grace in the blade become grace in the ear? Have we a deeper sense of the depravity of our nature? Are we more habitually looking out of self into Christ, and do we walk in closer fellowship with him? Let us answer these questions, and then remember the injunction of the apostle, 'See then that ye walk circumspectly, not as fools, but as wise, redeeming the time, because the days are evil.'

And now that the lion-standard of the tribe of Judah is uplifted for another march, let us confidently and joyously follow it. Jehovah is with us, and the God of Jacob is our refuge. Rise up, Lord, and let thine enemies be scattered; and let them that hate thee flee before thee! We shall tread upon them lion and adder; the young lion and the dragon shall we trample under our feet. 'They that wait upon the Lord shall renew their strength; they shall mount up with wings as eagles; they shall run, and not be weary; and they shall walk, and not faint.'

Letters of consolation

This cheering and helpful note was written to a lady who had told Mr Spurgeon of her many trials:

Westwood,
9 March, '81

Dear Friend,
You seem to me to be in the night school – by no means pleasant lessons, few holidays, and no cakes and sugar sticks but a wise Teacher, and guarantee of becoming a well-trained disciple in due time. This is much better than to be pampered with joyous excitements, and to be thereby really weakened in faith. How could you honour Christ, by trusting him as he is revealed in Scripture, if you were always having new revelations over and above his word? Too much sight renders faith impossible. A certain measure of darkness is needful for the full exercise of faith. Be of good comfort; for he who has redeemed you will not lose that which has cost him so much. I hope you will yet recover strength. Why, you are only a young girl yet at thirty-seven! But I know how the spirits sink, and one feels as old as Methuselah. The Lord be ever your Comforter!
    Yours, with much to do,
    C. H. Spurgeon

One of Mr Spurgeon's dearest and most intimate friends was Mr

William Higgs, the builder of the Tabernacle, and a deacon of the church worshipping there. The following extracts from letters to Mrs Higgs, when her dear husband was 'called home', will show how fully the pastor sympathized with her and the whole of the bereaved family:

Westwood,
3 January, 1883

Dear Friend,

How I wish that I could come and join you in your grief, even if I could not give you comfort! But I am too lame to move. Ah, me! What a blow! We were all afraid of it, but did not think it would come just now. Doubtless it is best as it is; but it is a sharp gash in the heart. He was a dear soul to us all, but specially to you. I beg the Lord to bear you up under this the heaviest of all trials . . . All is well *with him*. There is our comfort. His pains and wearinesses are over, and he rests. I will come as soon as I can travel, but this swollen right foot holds me like a fetter of iron.

Loving sympathy to every one of you. God bless you!

Yours ever heartily,

C. H. Spurgeon

Westwood,
6 January, 1883

Dear Mrs Higgs,

L. and G. have now told me all about our dear one's death. The Lord has dealt well with him. I wonder how he lived so long to cheer us all: and I feel relieved that he lived no longer, for it would have been great anguish to him. He has gone at the right time. The Lord will be your comfort and help. I meant to go to you this morning, but I found my foot would not let me go up and down steps. It is a double pain to be kept from you and your sorrowing family . . . We shall all meet again . . . Let us bless God. Can we?

Your loving friend,

C. H. Spurgeon

When Pastor T. W. Medhurst lost a daughter, Mr Spurgeon wrote to him:

Westwood,
24 May, 1884

Dear Friend,

May you be sustained under your heavy trial! Now that you and your dear companion are most fully realizing the void which is made in your household, may you find living consolations flowing into your hearts! 'It is well', and faith knows it is so; and worships the Lord from under the cloud. How time has flown! It seems but the other day that you were married; and now you are an old father, bereaved of a daughter. Dear Caleb Higgs, too, is gone home long ago.

We shall meet above before long. Till then, in our Lord's business we will find solace, and in himself delight.

Yours ever heartily,
C. H. Spurgeon

The following letter was written to an Oxfordshire clergyman with whom Mr Spurgeon had long been in close personal friendship:

Westwood,
12 June, 1884

Dear Friend,

I casually heard from Mr Abraham that you were ill, but I had no idea that it was a serious matter; but Mr Rochfort has kindly given me further news. I feel very sad about it, but I am sure you do not. The loss will be ours, and heaven and you will gain.

Dear loving brother, you have nothing now to do but to go home; and what a home! You will be quite at home where all is love, for you have lived in that blessed element, and are filled with it. I shall soon come hobbling after you; and shall find you out. We are bound to gravitate to each other whether here or in glory. We love the same Lord, and the same blessed truth.

May the everlasting arms be underneath you! I breathe for you a loving, tender prayer – 'Lord, comfort thy dear servant, and when he departs, may it be across a dried-up river into the land of living fountains!'

I am fifty next Thursday, and you are near your Jubilee. In this we are alike; but Jesus is the highest joy. Into the Father's hands I commit you, 'until the day break, and the shadows flee away'.

Your loving brother,

C. H. Spurgeon

Dear Mr Feltham,

It is a great sorrow to lose such a mother, but also a great joy to know it is well with her. She could not have passed away under happier circumstances. She must have been glad to see her son so happily settled, and then gladder still to be with her Lord for ever. No lingering sickness, no fierce pain; but gentle dismission, and instant admission into the glory. I envy her as much as I dare. The Lord be with you and your beloved, and comfort you to the full!

Your sympathizing friend,

C. H. Spurgeon

Mentone,
14 Dec., '87

Dear Mr Bartlett,

I sorrow with you over the departure of your little Lillie; but you will feel that there is honey with the gall. She was a dear child, ready to take her place with the shining ones. Grandmother will receive her as a messenger from you.

May peace and consolation flow into the heart of yourself and wife! I send you a little cheque to ease the expense. I cannot ease your pain; but there is 'another Comforter' who can and will do so. Receive my hearty sympathy. We are all going the same way. The little one has outrun us; we shall catch her up soon.

Yours very heartily,

C. H. Spurgeon

Westwood,
30 April, 1889

Dear Friend,

I heard with deep regret of your dear father's loss – which is your mother's gain. I do not wonder that the beloved man is not well. It is a crushing stroke, and he has a tender heart. The Lord himself sustain him! The Holy Spirit himself has undertaken the office of Comforter because there is such need of comfort in the tried family, and because it is such work as only God can do effectually. I commend you to the 'other Comforter'. I could not expect to see you at the College supper, but it is very kind of you to write me. You cheer me much by the reminder of the use of *The Cheque Book* to the dying one. God be praised!

I may send you my Christian love in this hour of sorrow, for I feel great sympathy with you and your father, and a hallowed oneness of heart with you in the faith of our Lord, and in service for his name. May a sweet hush fall on your hearts!

Yours very truly,
C. H. Spurgeon

A few months later, Dr Habershon also received the summons, 'Come up higher'. During his last illness, his daughter wrote to inform Mr Spurgeon, and he replied as follows:

Westwood,
3 Aug., 1889

Dear Friend,

You are now tried indeed, but all-sufficient grace will bear you through. I desire my tenderest love to your suffering father. If he is now going home, I congratulate him upon the vision which will soon burst upon him. If he tarries with us a little longer, it will be profitable for you. We have not the pain of choice. It is a great mercy that we are not placed in the perplexing dilemma of choosing either for ourselves or others, whether we live or die. I pray for you both. May you maintain the peace which now rules you, and find it even brightening into joy in the Lord's will! Jesus said to the women at the sepulchre, 'All hail'. All is well.

Yours most heartily,
C. H. Spurgeon

Mr Spurgeon's presence and address at the funeral greatly comforted the mourners; and in thanking him, Miss Habershon consulted him with regard to the future, and received the following reply:

Westwood,
6 Sept., 1889

Dear Friend,

It would seem to be wise advice which would lead your brother to take your father's house. In the profession, a measure of *prestige* is valuable, and this hangs even about the abode of a distinguished man when the name is the same. You and your sister will be rightly led, for you look up; and there is a finger which never misleads.

It is a great solace to be able to do anything to comfort your heart. Your thanks are far more than I deserve; but I did honestly endeavour to bear a testimony which I pray our Lord to impress on some for whom we felt anxious.

In these crises of life, the power to sit still is greater than that of activity – which frets into restlessness. I commend you to the Good Shepherd. HE will direct your path.

Yours very heartily,
C. H. Spurgeon

At one of the meetings during the College Conference of 1890, a very touching prayer was presented by Dr Usher, who pleaded with great earnestness for the salvation of the children of the brothers. The beloved President, Mr Spurgeon, was much moved by the petition, and the hearty response which it evoked; and he at once offered to write to all the ministers' sons and daughters whose fathers intimated their wish for him to do so by sending to him their children's names and ages.

My Dear Lily,

I was a little while ago at a meeting for prayer where a large number of ministers were gathered together. The subject of prayer was 'our children'. It soon brought tears to my eyes to hear those good fathers pleading with God for their sons and daughters. As they went on entreating the Lord to save their families, my heart seemed ready to burst with strong desire that it might be even so. Then I thought, I will write to those sons and daughters, and remind them of their parents' prayers.

Dear Lily, you are highly privileged in having a parent who prays for you. Your name is known in the courts of heaven. Your case has been laid before the throne of God.

Do you not pray yourself? If you do not do so, why not? If other people value your soul, can it be right for you to neglect it? All the entreaties and wrestlings of your father will not save you if you never seek the Lord yourself. You know this.

You do not intend to cause grief to dear and precious father: but you do. So long as you are not saved, his heart can never rest. However obedient, and sweet, and kind you may be, he will never feel happy about you until you believe in the Lord Jesus Christ, and so find everlasting salvation.

Think of this. Remember how much you have already sinned, and none can wash you but Jesus. When you grow up, you may become very sinful, and none can change your nature and make you holy but the Lord Jesus, through his Spirit.

You need what father so earnestly seeks for you, and you need it NOW. Why not seek it at once? I heard a father pray, 'Lord, save our children; *and save them young.*' It is never too soon to be safe; never too soon to be happy; never too soon to be holy. Jesus loves to receive the very young ones.

You cannot save yourself, but the great Lord Jesus can save you. Ask him to do it. 'He that asketh receiveth.' Then trust in Jesus to save you. He can do it, for he died and rose again that whosoever believeth in him might not perish, but have everlasting life. Come and tell Jesus you have sinned; seek forgiveness; trust in him for it, and be sure that you are saved.

Then imitate our Lord. Be at home what Jesus was at Nazareth. Jesus will be a happy home, and your dear father and other friends will feel that the dearest wish of their hearts has been granted them.

I pray you to think of heaven and hell; for in one of those places you will live for ever. *Meet me in heaven!* Meet me at once at the mercy-seat. Run upstairs and pray to the great Father, through Jesus Christ.

Yours very lovingly,
C. H. Spurgeon

Miscellaneous letters

Infant salvation

Among the many falsehoods which, at different times, were told concerning Mr Spurgeon, one which he naturally repelled with the utmost indignation was the statement that he once declared that 'there are in hell infants a span long'. In reply to a correspondent who asked if he had ever said this, he wrote:

Newington, S.E.
12 June, 1869

Dear Sir,
I have never, at any time in my life, said, believed, or imagined that any infant, in any circumstances, would be cast into hell. I have always believed in the salvation of all infants, and I intensely detest the opinions which your opponent dared to attribute to me. I do not believe that, on this earth, there is a single professing Christian holding the damnation of infants; or, if there be, he must be insane, or utterly ignorant of Christianity. I am obliged by this opportunity of denying the calumny, although the author of it will probably find

no difficulty in inventing some other fiction to be affirmed as unblushingly as the present one. He who doubts God's word is naturally much at home in slandering the Lord's servants.

Yours truly,
    C. H. Spurgeon

The question of the salvation of infants is also referred to in the following note, which was written to a minister whose infant child had died, and to whose wife a Christadelphian had expressed the idea that children dying at that age have no existence after death:

Clapham,
8 June, 1872

Dear Friend,

I am just leaving home and can only write and say – May the Comforter fulfil his divine office in your hearts! The child is with Jesus. David did not think his babe annihilated when he said, 'I shall go to him'. Away with these foolish dreams! The Lord be with you!

Yours in sympathy,
    C. H. Spurgeon

Part of a letter from Spurgeon to his mother

Dear Mother,

I need your prayers doubly at this time. I know I shall have them, and I believe I have felt the blessing of them more than once. The Lord visit you both, and bear you up in his everlasting arms! Troubles you have had, but I believe the comforts have always kept you joyful in tribulation; cast down, but not in despair.

Bless the Lord, I must say, for making me his son; 'tis of his own sovereign mercy. Not one good thing has failed. I have felt corruptions rise, and the old man is strong – but grace always comes in just at the critical time, and saves me from myself. The Lord keep me! I have no hope of going on well but by his power. I know that his almighty arm is all-sufficient. Get everyone you can to pray for me; a prayer is more precious than gold, it makes me rich. Lift up your arms, like Moses; there is a great battle both in me and out of me. Jesus intercedes; sweet thought, to one who needs just such a Pleader. Jehovah-Jesus, his people's buckler, is near; an ever-present help in time of trouble, not afar off. We live in him, he is all around us; who shall destroy his favourites, his darlings? I have had for one of my sermons, John 15:9 'As the Father hath loved me, so have I loved you: continue ye in my love.' Here is:

1 Love without beginning.	God never began to love Jesus.
2 Love without limit.	God loves Jesus with an unbounded love.
3 Love without change.	God always loved Jesus alike, equally.
4 Love without end.	When will God leave off loving Jesus?

Even so does Jesus love you and me.

How are all Christian friends? Love to Mr Langford, and my best respects; tell him I desire a special interest in his prayers. I want to feel 'less than nothing', but this is a very great attainment. Thank Father for his letter; the Lord of hosts prosper his labours abundantly! My very best love to yourself. I hope, if it is right, that your hands are well. Kiss the little ones, and give them my love. May they learn of Jesus! I am glad Arthur gets on so well; may your ten thousand prayers for us be answered by him that heareth prayer! Emily is stronger, I hope; ask her to think whether she loves Jesus with all her heart.

Love to you all once more, from your affectionate son.
　　Charles

Sermons in candles

The candle and the fly

In almost every collection of emblems, I have found the candle, and perhaps most frequently of all, *the candle and the fly*. Giles Corrozet's *Hecatomgraphie*, a French work dated 1540, gives the motto, *'War is sweet only to the inexperienced'*, with the picture of a number of moths or butterflies fluttering towards a candle: said candle and moths being of gigantic size if compared with the room. Attached to the woodcuts are verses which signify that only those who do not know its great dangers seek the battlefield. This reminds me that the good Earl of Shaftesbury told me that when he was Lord Ashley, he once rode with the Duke of Wellington through the lovely villages of Berkshire and for half an hour the warrior was silent. When at length he spoke, he said, 'I dare say you wonder what has made me so quiet. I was thinking of the havoc which war would make of all this peace and beauty. If we should ever come here, it might be my duty to burn and destroy all these happy homes. Whether there follows upon it defeat or victory, war is a great calamity.' The great soldier spoke the truth. May those nations which delight in war rest content with former burnings of their wings, and let the flame alone.

Others have used the same emblem as a warning against the indulgence of sinful passions. The motto is, 'short but ruinous pleasure'. 'For one pleasure a thousand pains.' The sin promised to enlighten the eyes, but it burned into the very soul. Full often when we hear of young people ruined by unbridled appetites, we are apt to say with the world's great poet –

> Thus hath the candle singed the moth.

Error has the same effect on certain restless minds. No sooner is a new theory started, than they make a dash for it; and though it costs them comfort, fellowship, and holiness, they fly at it again. 'O foolish Galatians, who hath bewitched you?' The fascination of novelty appears to be irresistible when minds are weak and conceited.

A picture of a candle

Think of a picture of a candle. In artistic circles the drawing of an object may cost far more than the object itself. Did not the Shah of Persia once ask the price of the painting of a donkey, and, when he heard the amazing demand, he calculated how many real asses could have been purchased with the money. No doubt a well-painted picture of a candle would cost as much as would light us for many a month, and yet it would never yield to our necessity a single beam of light. So, the resemblance of true godliness costs a man far more care and trouble than the genuine article would involve, and yet it is nothing after all. One cannot light himself to bed by the picture of a candle, neither can he find comfort in the hour of death by the imitation of religion. There must be reality, and that reality involves flame and light: in our case a flame and light which none but God can give. If there be nothing of heavenly fire and spiritual truth about our piety, our profession is vain. The great distinction between living grace and its imitation can be seen by all spiritual minds. We are overdone with portraits, but men are by no means plentiful. We have as many paintings of candles as the church walls will hold; but we have few real lamps, or else this world would not remain so dark as it now is. Those candles which are not consumed by their own flame are giving no light, and those persons who are themselves unaffected in heart and life by their religion may fear that they are mocking themselves with the mere appearance of sacred things. You may sit a long time in front of a painted fire before you will be warmed, and you may long maintain formal religion, and yet never derive comfort from it. To look for a lost ring in a dark cellar by the help of the picture of a candle is not more unreasonable than to look for rest of heart in a godliness which is a mere pretence.

A candle box

Our third emblem is not a candle, but a case for candles, a casket for those jewels of light. It is a candle box, well-fashioned and neatly japanned. At the back are two plates with holes in them by which to hang up the box against the wall. It closes very neatly, opens very readily, and keeps its contents out of harm's way. Within it are a number of the very best candles, from the most notable makers. Wax, stearine, palmatine, and so forth – there could not be a handsomer assortment. Let no one despise this: here we have capacity, elegance, preparation, and plenty of each. But suppose that we were in a room without the gas, and I were simply to exhibit the candle box and its contents, and say, 'Here is brilliance! You need no electric lighting: this box abundantly suffices for the enlightenment of this large assembly!' You would reply, 'But we see none the better for your boasted illumination. The candles are shut up in their box, and yield no single beam of light.' Herein detect a resemblance to many a church. We could readily find communities of Christian people who are shut up to themselves, and are without the living fire of the Spirit of God. What is the good of them?

This is a very respectable candle box; it could hardly be more respectable. Similarly, you may see a highly respectable congregation, very refined and select! The minister is a 'man of high culture and advanced thought'. He can confound a text of Scripture with any living man. He attracted at least five horses to his place of preaching last Sunday. They say it takes a great deal of ability to draw a horse to church! As for his hearers, they are all the cream of the cream. Don't you know that the doctor, and the brewer, and the lawyer, and the auctioneer all attend that most honoured sanctuary? What with an M.D. and a D.D. and an F.R.S., two wealthy dowagers, a Colonel, a County Councillor and a Professor, it is worth while for a fellow to go to that chapel – I beg pardon – *church*, for the sake of the social distinction which it will bestow upon him. The people are so very respectable that they do not know one another, and never think of shaking hands. They are all so very select that they float about in distinguished isolation, like so many icebergs in the Atlantic. The families walk up the aisles with the most becoming dignity, and they walk down the aisles with the most proper decorum. They can do without warmth, brotherly love, sympathy, and co-operation; for their eminent 'respectability' suffices for every need. Of course, they can do nothing more; for it costs them all their time, talent, thought, and spare cash to maintain their superior respectability. Like the gentleman with his well-brushed hat, no wonder that they look so superior, for they give their whole minds to it.

One asked a member of a certain respectable church whether he taught in a Ragged School, and *really* he could hardly answer the fellow. The superior person champed the word 'Ragged School' as a donkey might a roll of oakum. Another, a portly deacon, was asked whether he would join in holding an open-air service; but he looked the intruder through and through as if he would like to open *him*. None of the ladies and gentlemen help the Temperance work, for they are too respectable to go in with vulgar water drinkers; neither do they visit the lodging houses, for that would be too disreputable for their royal highnesses. All these make up an eminently respectable community; but why they are respected, this deponent is not saying.

Here, take away this candle box! I want no more of it or its contents, for it gives no jot of light! That is what will happen to very respectable churches which do no work for God or man: they will be put away, and even their candlestick will be taken out of its place. If they do not mend their ways, not a few of our dissenting churches will die out, and leave nothing behind them but a name to laugh at. A church which does nothing for those around it, mocks the need of men, leaves the world in darkness, and grieves the Lord who designed his people to be the lights of the world.

As in a community, so with a single person; grace is essential to usefulness. All the candles in that box remain useless till the wick is lighted with a touch of fire. If I bring one unlit candle in contact with another, they are tête-à-tête, or wick-à-wick, but the first has no influence upon the second. A thousand such interviews will produce no result. If there were a living flame, you could soon set not only that one candle shining, but as many as you chose to bring; but without it nothing can be done. No man can communicate what he has not got: you cannot hope to save your fellow-man till you know the salvation of God for yourself. To be a preacher or teacher before one has received the divine life is as foolish as for a candle to set up as a lighter of others before it has been lighted itself. How different the result when the living flame is there, and one sets the other ablaze at once!

An array of (unlit) candles

Variety is charming, and number is cheering. The more the merrier, and especially of such reputable and notable light-givers as these. We may consider that we are having quite an illumination. With so many luminaries we need hardly regret the sunset. But is it so? I, for one, am none the better for these promising lights. I put on my spectacles – but there is no improvement. I can see nothing; and yet there are candles enough and to spare! There is no mystery about it – the candles are not lighted, and until they are lighted they cannot remove our darkness. Grace is needed to make gifts available for the service of God.

Let us look more closely into our collection of lights. Here is one which I should suppose to be an archbishop at the least. This other specimen is a Doctor of Divinity. *These* are gentry, and these are merchants, and those are 'cultured' individuals; but without the light from on high they are all equally unserviceable. A poor converted lad in a workshop will be of more spiritual use than a parliament of unregenerate men.

A lighted rushlight

I introduce you to a lighted rushlight, and there is more to be seen by this ignoble luminary than by all the rest. Little ability, set on fire by the life of God, may produce greater results than ten talents without the divine power. 'A living dog is better than a dead lion'; a zealous but illiterate Christian may be worth twenty lifeless philosophers.

There is great encouragement in this, dear friends: if you once get a light, it will spread from one to another without end. This one lighted candle would suffice to set a hundred candles shining. It may light a much finer candle than itself. Fire is one of those things for which there is no accounting as to what may come of it. Its spread is not to be measured even by leagues when it once gets firm hold, and the wind drives it on. Piety in a cottage may enlighten a nation. If the church of God were reduced to one person, it might, within an incredibly short time, become a great multitude.

There is a true apostolical succession in the kingdom of grace. Office has the pretence of it, but grace gives the reality. At Mr Jay's Jubilee, Timothy East, of Birmingham, told how, by the youthful ministry of William Jay, a thoughtless youth was converted and became a minister. Under the preaching of that man, Timothy East himself was led to repentance; and then by a sermon from Timothy East, John Williams, who became the martyr of Erromanga and the apostle of the South Sea Islands, was savingly impressed. See how the light goes from Jay to another, from that other to East, from East to Williams, and from Williams to the savages of the Southern Seas!

A family tree of an equally interesting character has been traced with regard to books as surely as with living witnesses for God. A Puritan tract, old and torn, was lent by a poor man to Baxter's father. It was called *Bunny's Resolutions*. Through reading this little book, Richard Baxter, afterward the great preacher of

Kidderminster, received a real change of heart. Baxter wrote *The Saint's Everlasting Rest*, which was blessed to the conversion of Doddridge. He wrote *The Rise and Progress*, which was the means of the conversion of Legh Richmond, and he wrote his *Dairyman's Daughter*, which has been translated into more than fifty languages, and has led to the conversion of thousands of souls. How many of these converted ones have in their turn written books and tracts which have charmed others to Jesus, eternity alone will reveal. We can never see the issues of our acts. We may strike a match, and from that little flame a street may be lighted. Give a light to your next door neighbour, and you may be taking the nearest way to instruct the twentieth century, or to send the Gospel to Chinese Tartary, or to overthrow the popular science fetish of the hour. A spark from your kitchen candle may, in its natural progression from one to another, light the last generation of men; so the word of the hour may be the light of the age, by which men may come in multitudes to see their Saviour and Lord. Let thy light shine, and what will come of it thou shalt see hereafter.

Coming one Thursday in the late autumn from an engagement beyond Dulwich, my way led up to the top of the Herne Hill ridge. I came along the level out of which rises the steep hill I had to ascend. While I was on the lower ground, riding in a hansom cab, I saw a light before me, and when I came near the hill, I marked that light gradually go up the hill, leaving a train of stars behind it. This line of new-born stars remained in the form of one lamp, and then another, and another. It reached from the foot of the hill to its summit. I did not see the lamplighter. I do not know his name, nor his age, nor his residence; but I saw the lights which he had kindled, and these remained when he himself had gone his way. As I rode along, I thought to myself, 'How earnestly do I wish that my life may be spent in lighting one soul after another with the sacred flame of eternal life! I would myself be as much as possible unseen while at my work, and would vanish into the eternal brilliance above when my work is done.' Will you, my brother, begin to light up some soul tonight? Speak of Jesus to some person who does not know him. Who can tell but you may save a soul from death? Then carry the flame to another, and to another. Mark the years of your life by your continual diligence in spreading 'the light of the knowledge of the glory of God in the face of Jesus Christ'.

A taper to light a candle
The taper which I hold in my hand is in itself a poor thing as an illuminator, but it has created quite a splendour in the room by the light which it has communicated to others. Andrew was not a very great personage, but he called his brother Peter, and led him to Jesus, and Peter was a host in himself. Never mind how small a taper you may be; burn on, shine at your best, and God bless you. You may lead on to grand results despite your feebleness. Those holy women who talked together as they sat in the sun at Bedford were a blessing to John Bunyan; but we do not know the name of even one of them. Everywhere the hidden ones are used by the Lord as the means of lighting up those who shine as stars in the churches.

In the service of God we find the greatest expansion of our being. It makes the dead man speak, and it also makes a single living man spread himself over a province. Our forefathers were fond of riddles. I cannot say that they were very witty ones, but there was solidity in them. Here is one – What is that of which twenty could be put into a tankard, and yet one would fill a barn? Twenty candles unlighted would scarcely fill a jug; but one when it is lighted will beneficially fill a barn with light, or viciously fill it with fire and smoke. A man, what is he? A man of God, what is he not? Our influence may enlighten the world and shine far down the ages, if the Holy Spirit's fire kindles us.

An unlit candle without a candlestick
Here is a candle which has never given any light yet, and never will as it is now. Hear its reason for not giving light: it is so unfortunate that it cannot find a proper candlestick in which to stand upright and fulfil the purpose for which it was made. Let us try to

accommodate it. Here is a fine church candlestick, and we set our candle in the socket. Does it shine? No. Shall we try a lower place? It does not shine any better. We will put this candle in the most enviable position – in a real silver candlestick, of the most elaborate workmanship. It does not shine one whit the more. Neither high nor low places will make a man what he is not.

I know people who cannot get on anywhere; but, according to their own belief, the fault is not in themselves, but in their surroundings. I could sketch you a brother who is unable to do any good because all the churches are so faulty. He was once with us, but he came to know us too well, and grew disgusted with our dogmatism and lack of taste. He went to the Independents who have so much more culture, breadth, and liberality. He grew weary of what he called 'cold dignity'. He wanted more fire, and therefore favoured the Methodists with his patronage. Alas, he did not find them the flaming zealots he had supposed them to be: he very soon outgrew both them and their doctrines, and joined our most excellent friends, the Presbyterians. These proved to be by far too high and dry for him, and he became rather sweet upon the Swedenborgians, and would have joined them had not his wife led him among the Episcopalians. Here he might have taken it easy with admirable propriety; and have even grown into a church-warden; but he was not content; and before long I heard that he was an Exclusive Brother! There I leave him, hoping that he may be better in his new line than he has ever been in the old ones.

The same illustration suggests to me to ask you whether you know the young man who cannot serve God as an apprentice, but is going to do wonders when he is out of his time? Yes, he only wants to be put into another candlestick. So he thinks: but we know better. When he is out of his time, and has become a journeyman, he will postpone his grand plans of usefulness till he has started as a master on his own account. Alas, when he is a master, he will wait till he has made money and can retire from business. So, you see, the candle does not shine, but it imputes its failure to the candle-sticks! The candlesticks are not to be blamed.

Poor Dick Miss-the-Mark believes that he ought to have been Oliver Cromwell; but as that character is hardly in season this year of grace, Richard is unable to be Cromwell, and therefore he is not himself at all. That wart over the eye, and other Cromwellian distinctions, are a dead loss in his case. He cannot develop his genius for lack of a King Charles and a Prince Rupert. The proper candlestick is not forthcoming, and so this fine candle cannot shine.

A 'self-fitting' candle

This is a very simple affair – Field's Self-fitting Candle; but it is very handy. You see, owing to the shape of its lower end, the candle will fit into any candlestick, whether it be large or small. A man of this sort makes himself useful anywhere. In poverty he is content; in wealth he is humble. Put him in a village, and he instructs the ignorant; place him in a city, he seeks the fallen. If he can preach, he will do so; and if that is beyond his capacity, he will teach in the Sabbath school. Like the holy missionary Brainerd, if he cannot convert a tribe, he will, even on his dying bed, be willing to teach a poor child his letters. It is a great thing not only to be able to fit in to all kinds of work, but to cope with all sorts of people. The power of adaptation to high and low, learned and ignorant, sad and frivolous, is no mean gift. If, like Nelson, we can lay our vessel side by side with the enemy, and come to close quarters without delay, we shall do considerable execution. Commend me to the man who can avail himself of any conversation, and any topic, to drive home saving truth upon the conscience and heart. He who can ride a well-trained horse, properly saddled, does well; but the fellow who can leap upon the wild horse of the prairie, and ride him barebacked, is a genius indeed. 'All things to all men,' rightly interpreted, is a motto worthy of the great apostle of the Gentiles, and of all who, like him, would win souls for Jesus.

It is a pity when a man is too big for his position – as some candles are too big to fit in certain candlesticks. Don't I know some Jacks-in-office who are a world too great to be of the slightest use to

164

anybody? Don't ask them a question unless you desire to be eaten up alive. On the other hand, it is not pretty to see a candle with paper round it to keep it in its place; nor is it nice to see a little man padded out to make him fill up an important office. Some men in prominent positions are like the small boy on the high horse; they need a deal of holding on. Be fit for your office, or find one for which you are fit. It is not a very great invention to make a candle self-fitting, but the result is very pleasant. Though the expression, 'the right man in the right place', is said to be a tautology, I like it, and I like it best of all to see it in actual life. Try to fit yourself to whatever comes in your way.

A candle stuck in a bottle
Hearty service, rendered from pure motives, is acceptable to God, even when people of education and taste have just cause to find fault with its imperfections. If we cannot bear witness for the Gospel in grammatical language, we may be thankful that we can do it at all, and we may be encouraged by the questionable fact that God blesses the most unsophisticated utterances. When you go to do a bit of carpentering in the shed, and need a light, you are sometimes on the look-out for the means of setting up your bit of candle in a handy way. The great invention in which your researches usually end is to stick a candle into a ginger-beer bottle, and the light which comes from it is quite as clear as if it were in a fine plated candlestick. Here is a popular implement, and it is both handy and cheap. Who would find any fault with it if he were in the dark, and wanted to find something in a hurry? If you have no fitter candlestick, a ginger-beer bottle does mightily well. How often our Lord has used men of scanty education, or of none at all! How useful he has made the things which are despised! Yet, at the same time, if it were left to me to make my choice as to how I would have my candle set up, I should not object to have it in a more presentable stand. I would not quarrel even if the candle given to me to go to bed with were in a silver candlestick. For use I would sooner have a ginger-beer bottle with a bright candle in it than a

plated candlestick with a dead candle in it which I could not light. Who would object to be rid of the guttering and the hot dropping tallow, and to handle a concern which would not dirty his hands? A thing of beauty and of brightness is a joy for ever. Grace shines none the less because the person and his speech are graceful. The world, with its Board Schools, is getting more and more educated, and the rage for ginger-beer-bottle lights is not so great as it was. We have now passed beyond the age in which vulgarity and power were supposed to be nearly related. As there is no sin, that I know of, in grammatical language and good taste, I hope we shall never set a fictitious value upon coarseness, nor go out of our way to marry godliness with slang. Our Lord and his cause should be served with our best. Even our best is not of itself worthy of his glory; but at least let us not give to him the offal and the refuse of human speech. Young man, blaze away; but you need not be coarse. Bring us a light, but use a decent candlestick if you can.

A number of very small candles on a board

Some excellent people have very little talent indeed. It is not merely that there is a want of education, but there is a want of capacity. Now, when that happens to be the case, my next illustration may be a serviceable hint. Imagine that we have fixed a number of very small candles on a board; and as they are all well alight, the result is by no means unsatisfactory. As a company of illuminators they make a pleasant and notable shining, and I note that the children present are greatly pleased with their brightness. Let us observe how a number of good little people, well lighted by grace, can, by combination, really give out a great deal more illumination than far greater people who shine alone. If one of you cannot do much in a place by yourself, look up other friends, start a Sunday school, and all of you work together. You may do great things by earnest unity. Form a little army for preaching in the street. Band together to visit from house to house. Scatter tracts over the whole area by concerted action. Unity is light. Even children, youths, and maidens may make a great blaze by working together in the holy cause. But you must each one of you shine your quota, and no one must try to save his candle, and take things easy. All at it, and always at it, and you will not labour in vain. A great ecclesiastical candle has never given a tenth of the light of thee little instruments; nor would he, I fear, if I were now to set him burning. The unanimous services of the lesser members of our churches might suffice to light up our country, and the world itself, by the blessing of God.

An unused candle

Imagine a candle hanging on the wall, all mouldy and perishing. It may serve as a striking likeness of those who have done nothing for their God, or for their fellow-men. It is better to be consumed in shining than to perish ignominiously in doing nothing. I need scarcely quote the old proverb, 'It is better to wear out than to rust out'. Idleness is a destroyer. For every evil brought upon us by excessive labour, ten will come to us by laziness. Our accidents happen in our holidays. When the pot is not boiling the flies will come to it. Mice will not nibble a lighted candle, but when the fire is gone, they find tallow a rather toothsome article. Who cares to be eaten by mice? Who wishes to die of the miserables? Who would like to be eaten up with whims, or nibbled away by crotchets? If we have no such desire, let us accept that sacred fire which will cause us to yield up our whole being to the hallowed purpose of light-giving. For this we are kept in this dark world. We must be burning and shining lights, or we miss our vocation. Truly, he that saves his life loses it, and only he who spends his life for God shall find it unto life eternal.

Candle on a headband

Butchers, it seems, are accustomed to do their work with a candle fastened upon their foreheads with a band around their heads. There is an old story of one who had lost his candle, and travelled all round his premises searching for it by its own light. It is told as a jest, and it must have been a mirthful incident where it happened. I remember an old gentleman who could see very little without spectacles, but went up and down the house searching for his glasses, looking through them all the time. The parable is this: a person full of doubts and fears about his personal condition before God is searching for grace within, by the light of that very grace for which he is looking. He is fearfully anxious because he can see no trace of gracious anxiety in his mind. He feels sad because he cannot feel sad. He repents because he cannot repent. He has the candle on his forehead, and is seeing by the light of it, and yet he is searching for that very light, without which he could not search at all. Many a time a man laments that he does not feel, and all the while he is overwhelmed with pain through the impression that he does not feel pain as he should.

A common lantern

The wind may blow on a common lantern, but the candle is safe within. The groom can cross the stable-yard in a shower of rain, or in a fall of snow, when his light is thus safeguarded. On board ship also, the lantern is of the utmost use; for even a gale of wind will not blow out the candle which is secure in a good lantern.

The providence of God is the great protector of our life and usefulness, and under the divine care we are perfectly safe from every danger. Yet we are apt to complain of the very providence which blesses us. Years ago a farmer returned from market with a golden burden, for he had sold his corn. He thought it hard that it should rain and spoil his best coat; but when he came to the lone place between the woods, and perceived that a highwayman would have shot him if the rain had not damped his powder, he had a much more vivid idea of the wisdom of God.

Bernard Gilpin

Remember Bernard Gilpin, the apostle of the North. He was seized and taken to London to be tried as a heretic. On the road he fell from his horse, and broke his leg. His persecutors knew that he used to say, 'It is all for the best', so they taunted him with the enquiry, 'Is this all for the best?' And he meekly replied that he had no doubt it would turn out to be so.

Gilpin was right. A delay was caused on the road, and he and his guard arrived in London just as Queen Mary died. They heard the bells ringing when they came to Highgate Hill, and learned that Queen Elizabeth was on the throne. He was too late to be burned: he had broken his leg, but he had escaped the flames. In some way or other the Lord will preserve his people from all evil, just as the lantern preserves the light which is placed within it.

A candle under a bushel

Let me set before you an admirable illustration, which is not one of my own, but comes from the great Master of assemblies. Here is a candle, and of course we have brought it with a view to its giving light, but the absurd action that I am bent on is to cover it up with a bushel. It would be a very ridiculous thing to be at the pains of providing a lighted candle and then to hide it under a bushel. Yet I will do so to make the folly apparent to you all. I notice that you laugh; and well you may. You may use a bushel and use a candle; but by putting the candle under the bushel you use neither of them, but *mis*use both. I am sure none of you would be guilty of such an absurd action. And can it be that even a single person here would be so profane as to believe that the All-wise God would do that which we all condemn as folly? And yet, when those of you who have grace in your hearts profess to believe that you are placed where you can do no good, you virtually charge the Lord with lighting a candle and putting it under a bushel.

There is my respected brother, a working man. Hear what he has to say:

'My dear Mr Spurgeon, you cannot expect me to be doing any work in the church, for my daily labour leaves me no time for anything else. I could call the larks up in the morning; I am often abroad before the world is properly aired. Moreover, I have to work much too late to leave me a spare hour. I am willing, but quite unable to do a hand's turn for my Lord.'

Yes, yes, I see; you have to complain of a bushel which hides your light. God has lighted you, and then has put you where your light is

169

condemned to be unseen. Do you quite believe that it is so? Have you no suspicion that, after all, you could shine, if you were exceedingly anxious to do so?

'There!' cries another. 'I have little patience with a man who talks in that fashion; but as for me, I have hundreds of men to look after, and a great going concern, involving large capital, and this requires the whole of my energy both by day and by night. My cares are never over. Mine is brain-work of the most exhausting sort, and when I get away from the mill I feel no soul for reading, or prayer, or working in the cause of God. If it were hand labour, I should like the change to mental work; but I cannot keep on for ever thinking, or I shall, soon wear out my brain.'

Just so, my friend: God has given you the light of his grace, and has then deliberately placed a great golden bushel over the top of you! Do you feel sure that it is so? Is there not a still small voice, which whispers that there is something wrong?

But my friend Mrs. Fruitful, over there, says:

'I quite agree with you, sir. These people are not tied to their homes as I am, for I have eleven children; and what can I do? I have a great deal more to do than you men dream of; and it is not fiction that a mother's work is never ended. If anyone can plead a good excuse from the Lord's work, I am sure I can.'

Good sister, I sympathize with you, far more than with those who have already spoken. You have your share of life's burden in your large little family. It is true, eleven is better than so very many; but I have no doubt they are a handful, a lapful, and a heartful. Yet, surely, it cannot be quite true that you are altogether denied the pleasure of shining for your Lord; also it would seem as if he had kindled you as his own candle, and then had put you under the bushel of a large family, to prevent your shining.

Yet there is the candle, and there is the bushel. We cannot image that the bushel is to be on top of the candle. Still, they must be in some relation to each other. If we must not put the candle under the bushel, would it be amiss to put the bushel under the candle? See how well it looks! It is an admirable idea! Let us carry out its principle! Cannot the working man talk to his mates, and be a witness for Jesus in the shop? Parsons are all very well, but holy artisans can carry the truth where we have no entrance! Cannot the great manufacturer see to the interests of those whom he employs, and treat them, not as 'hands', but as souls? Might he not do a world of good among his mill people if he had but a mind? I think so. And you, good mother of those dozen children save one, surely you have a work ready to hand in your own house. What a splendid Sunday-school you have at home! Your children could not have a better teacher; and, from what little I know of them, I should say that you could not have much finer children to instruct. You will not be forced to walk weary miles to get to your class, nor will you be tempted to neglect your house; you can stay at home and train for God valuable church members, fine workers among the poor, and soul-winning missionaries for the home and foreign field. What nobler work can there be than that of a mother among her own little ones? See how, by being set upon the bushel, the candle stands in a place of vantage, and obtains a worthy pedestal from which to spread its light far and wide! Wisely used, that which would hinder the idle will assist the diligent. This is one of the feats of faith, to turn difficulties into helps, to slay the lion and find honey in his carcass, and thus, on stepping-stones of growing victory, rise to complete triumphs.

If there is real light in a man, you cannot keep him under a bushel. You may try to repress a man of talent, but he finds his level in due time. You may endeavour to destroy real grace when you meet with it among men; but neither your nor the devil will succeed. If you manage to place the gracious soul under a sort of bushel, something will happen for which you were not looking. If there is the real life of God within the person who is despised and covered up, the flame will find out a way for the revelation of the light. Grace may be oppressed; but it cannot be suppressed. In fact, it may be said of persecuted believers as of Israel in Egypt, 'The more they afflicted them, the more they multiplied and grew'.

A night-light

This is not technically called a candle, but in effect it is one. A night-light is a delightful invention for the sick. It has supplanted the rushlight, which would frequently be set in a huge sort of tower, which, to me, as a sick child at night, used to suggest dreadful things. With its light shining through the round holes at the side, like so many ghostly eyes, it looked at me sparingly; and with its round ring on the ceiling, it made me think of Nebuchadnezzar's burning fiery furnace. The night-light is so mild and quiet that it suits our weakness, and yet cheers our gloom. Blessed be the Child who first thought of it! Does it not remind you of a good, tender nurse? I always say – as a fine specimen of what I mean – my wife. She tells me that I cannot say this of her now, as she is so great an invalid; but I can speak of what she has been, and would be now if strength sufficed. She has been far more than a night-light to me in hours of pain. She moves across the room like the ancient deities, who were said to float rather than to walk. What gentle grace and tenderness! What unwearied watchfulness all through the night!

Honoured among women be the memory of Florence Nightingale! Her name and fame gave an impetus to the movement for trained nurses, which has been so fraught with comfort to thousands. Our young ladies who devote themselves to this sacred service deserve all the encouragement we can give them. God bless you, gentle night-lights!

Our night-light is set in water to make it quite safe. We do well to guard ourselves against the personal danger of our position: even when doing good we must be on our watch lest we fall into temptation.

Night-lights are marked to burn just so many hours, and no more; and so are we. Long may you each one shine and yield comfort to those around you; but, whether your hours be few or many, may you burn steadily to the end! If we may but fulfil our mission it will be enough. May none of us take fire in a wrong way, blaze into a shameful notoriety, fill the air with an ill savour, and then go out in darkness before half our work is done!

In the next similitude you have a simple reminder of the imperfections to which men are liable. A candle needs snuffers, and men need chastisement; for they are both of them subject to infirmity. In the temple of Solomon there were snuffers and snuff-dishes; but *they were all of gold*. God's rebukes are in love, and so should ours be: holy reproofs in the spirit of affection are snuffers of gold. Never use any other, and use even these with discretion, lest you put out the flame which it is your aim to improve. Never reprove in anger. Do not deal with a small fault as if it were a great crime. If you see a fly on your boy's forehead, don't try to kill it with a sledge-hammer, or you may kill the boy also. Do the needful but very difficult work of reproof in the kindest and wisest style, so that the good you aim at may be attained.

It was a shocking habit of bad boys to snuff the candle, and then open the snuffers and let the smoke and the smell escape. The snuffers are made on purpose to remove the snuff, or consumed wick, and then to quench it by pressure, and prevent any offensive smoke; but young urchins of a mischievous sort would set the snuffers wide and let the filthy smoke fill the room with its detestable odour. So do some who hear of a brother's faults, make them known, and seem to take pleasure in filling society with unsavoury reports. I pray you, do not do so. If the candle has something wrong with it, touch it carefully, snuff it with discretion, and shut up the obnoxious matter very carefully. Let us be silent about things which are a discredit to Christian character. Keep an ill report secret; and do not be like the young lady who called in a dozen friends to help her keep a secret, and yet, strange to say, it got out. Remember, you may yourself deserve rebuke one of these days; and as you would like this to be done gently and privately, so keep your remarks upon others within the happy circle of tender love. To rebuke in gentle love is difficult, but we must aim at it till we grow proficient. Golden snuffers, remember; only *golden* snuffers. Put away those old rusty things – those unkind sarcastic remarks. They will do more harm than good, and they are not fit things to be handled by servants of the Lord Jesus.

An upside-down candle

It cannot be long before an upside-down candle puts itself out. When in our hearts the lower nature is uppermost, and the animal dominates the spiritual, the flame of holy light cannot be kept alight long. When the world is uppermost, and eternal things have a low place in the heart, the sacred life is in serious jeopardy. When the intellect crushes down the affections, the soul is not in an upright state. It needs that matters be quickly righted, or the worse consequences must ensure. Our prayer should rise to God that this happen not to ourselves; and when we see that it is so with others, we should be full of prayerful concern that they may be turned by the hand of God into a true and upright condition.

Some men who are not quite upright waste much of their influence. To such we might apply the old and almost obsolete word – *candle-waster*. It is a pity to lose life in harmful or unprofitable ways.

The fat candle

Here is a very important-looking candle. Its dimensions are aldermanic. You expect great things from so portly an illuminator. Look at the size of it. But when I light it, the illuminating power is very small. Can you see any light coming from it? It is a star of the smallest magnitude. We have here the maximum of tallow and the minimum of light. The fact is that only a little of the fat just near the centre ever gets melted. This makes a little well of hot grease, but the rest is as hard and cold as if there were no burning wick in the middle. Thus it is with men of more talent than heart: the chief part of them is never used. Many a great and learned minister, with any quantity of Latin and Greek tallow, is but very little useful because his ability is not touched by his heart. Many a great, rich man, with any amount of the fat of wealth, never get warmed through: he is melted to the extent of a shilling or two, but his thousands are unaffected. Partial consecration is a very doubtful thing; and yet how much we have of it! What is wanted is 'grace more abundant', to fuse the whole man, and make every part and parcel of him subservient to God's great design of light-giving.

174

A cobbler's candle

The main business is to have plenty of heart. I have noticed that speakers produce an effect upon their audiences rather in proportion to their hearts than their heads. I was present at a meeting where a truly solid and instructive speaker succeeded in mesmerizing us all, so that in another half-minute we should all have been asleep. His talk was as good as gold, and as heavy. He was followed by a gentleman who was 'all there', what there was of him. He was so energetic that he broke a chair, and made us all draw in our feet for fear he should come down upon our corns. How the folks woke up! The galleries cheered him to the echo. I do not know what it was all about, and did not know at the time; but it was very wonderful. An express at sixty miles an hour is nothing to that orator. He swept past us like – well, like nothing at all. He meant it, and we felt that he deserved to be cheered for such zealous intentions. He was all ablaze, and we were willing for a season to rejoice in his light. I do not hold him up as an example, for in warfare we need shot as well as powder; but I could not help seeing that a warm heart and an energetic manner will carry the day where a cold ponderosity effects nothing. My friend was like a cobbler's candle with two wicks. His blaze was very large in proportion to the material which sustained it.

In our labour to do good we must not let our learning remain cold and useless. Dr Manton was one of the best of preachers, being both instructive and simple. On one occasion, however, he preached before an assembly of the great, and he very naturally used a more learned style than usual. He felt greatly rebuked when a poor man plucked him by the gown and lamented that, whereas he had often been fed under his ministry, there had been nothing for him on that occasion. The fire had not been so fierce as the tallow had been cold. It is a dreadful thing when hearers have more use for a dictionary than for a Bible under a sermon. A preacher may pile books on his head and heart till neither of them can work. Give me rather the enthusiastic Salvationist bearing a burning testimony, than your cultured philosopher prosing with chill propriety.

A candle burning at both ends

The next illustration is a warning, and not an example. You have often heard it said of such and such a person, 'he is burning the candle at both ends'. Spendthrifts waste both capital and interest; and by both neglecting business and wasting their substance on expensive pleasures, they burn the candle at both ends. The vicious not only exhaust their daily strength, but they draw upon the future of their constitutions, so that when a few years have gone they are old men before their time. Beware of burning the candle at both ends. It will go fast enough if you burn it only at one end; for your stock of strength and life is very limited. If there is anyone here who is sinning on the right hand and on the left, let him forbear, and not be in such fearful haste to endless ruin. Let this candle cast a light upon the folly of prodigality, and may the prodigal hasten home before his candle is burned out. Did you ever see a candle used in that way? You do not live with folks so mad; but if you look about you in the wide world, you may see how thousands are squandered and lives are cut short by burning the candle at both ends.

Some people are unreasonable towards ministers and evangelists, and want them to be worked to death. Many a valuable man of God has been lost to the church by his burning his candle at both ends.

A chandelier

We will conclude as they do at open-air entertainments – with the greatest display of our fireworks.

Here are many candles uniting their brilliance; they all hang upon one support, and shine by the same light. May they not represent the church of Christ in its multiplicity, variety, and unity? These candles are all supported upon one stem, they are all giving forth the same light, and yet they are of all manner of sorts, sizes, and colours. A great way off they would seem to be but one light. They are many, and yet but one. I happened one evening to say that nobody could tell which was the 'U.P.', and which was the

176

Free Church, or which was the Wesleyan, or the Primitive, or the Salvation Army, or the Baptists, and so on; but one strong old Baptist assured me that the 'Dips' gave the best light. Another said the Presbyterians were, on the whole, cast in the best mould; and a third thought the Church of England was made of the truest wax. I told them that some of the Baptists would be the better if they had another Baptism. The Free Churches might be none the worse for being more established in the faith; and even the Methodists might improve their methods. The main question is possession of the one light and fire of God, the flame of divine truth. Those who shine by divine grace are all one in Christ Jesus.

What a glory will there be in the one church when all her members shine, and all are one! May such a day come quickly! Amen.

Have I not proved that a world of illustration may be found in a candle?

Commenting and commentaries

Commentators

In order to be able to expound the Scriptures, and as an aid to your pulpit studies, you will need to be familiar with the commentators: a glorious army, let me tell you, whose acquaintance will be your delight and profit. Of course, you are not such wiseacres as to think or say that you can expound Scripture without assistance from the works of divines and learned men who have laboured before you in the field of exposition. If you are of that opinion, pray remain so, for you are not worth the trouble of conversion, and like a little coterie who think with you, would resent the attempt as an insult to your infallibility. It seems odd that certain men who talk so much of what the Holy Spirit reveals to themselves should think so little of what he has revealed to others. My chat this afternoon is not for these great originals, but for you who are content to learn from holy men, taught by God, and mighty in the Scriptures.

It has been the fashion in recent years to speak against the use of commentaries. If there were any fear that the expositions of Matthew Henry, Gill, Scott, and others would be exalted into Christian Targums, we would join the chorus of objectors, but the existence or approach of such a danger we do not suspect. The temptations of our times lie rather in empty pretensions to novelty of sentiment, than in a slavish following of accepted guides. A respectable acquaintance with the opinions of the giants of the past might have saved many an erratic thinker from wild interpretations and outrageous inferences. Usually, we have found the despisers of commentaries to be men who have no sort of acquaintance with them; in their case, it is the opposite of familiarity which has bred contempt. It is true there are a number of expositions of the whole Bible which are hardly worth shelf-room; they aim at too much and fail altogether; the authors have spread little learning over a vast surface, and have badly attempted for the entire Scriptures what they might have accomplished for one book with tolerable success; but who will deny the pre-eminent value of such expositions as those of Calvin, Ness, Henry, Trapp, Poole, and Bengel, which are as deep as they are broad? And yet further, who can pretend to biblical learning who has not made himself familiar with the great writers who spent a life in explaining some one sacred book? Caryl on Job will not exhaust the patience of a student who loves every letter of the Word; even Collinges, with his nine hundred and nine pages upon one chapter of the Song, will not be too full for the preacher's use; nor will Manton's long-metre edition of the hundred and nineteenth Psalm be too profuse. No stranger could imagine the vast amount of real learning to be found in old commentaries like the following: Durham on Solomon's Song, Wilcocks on Psalms and Proverbs, Jermin on Ecclesiastes and Proverbs, Greenhill on Ezekiel, Burroughs on Hosea, Ainsworth on the Pentateuch, King on Jonah, Hutcheson on John, Peter Martyr on Romans, etc., and in Willet, Sibbes, Bayne, Elton, Byfield, Daille, Adams, Taylor, Barlow, Goodwin, and others on the various epistles. Without attempting to give in detail the names of all, I intend in a familiar talk to mention the more notable, who wrote upon the whole Bible, or on either Testament, and I especially direct your attention to the titles, which in Puritan writers generally give in brief the run of the work.

Matthew Henry

First among the mighty for general usefulness we are bound to mention the man whose name is a household word, Matthew Henry. He is most pious and pithy, sound and sensible, suggestive and sober, terse and trustworthy. You will find him to be glittering with metaphors, rich in analogies, overflowing with illustrations, superabundant in reflections. He delights in apposition and alliteration; he is usually plain, quaint, and full of pith; he sees right through a text directly; apparently he is not critical, but he quietly gives the result of an accurate critical knowledge of the original fully up to the best critics of his time. He is not versed in the manners and customs of the East, for the Holy Land was not so accessible as in our day; but he is deeply spiritual, heavenly, and profitable; finding good matter in every text, and from all deducing most practical and judicious lessons. His is a kind of commentary to be placed where I saw it, in the old meeting-house at Chester – chained in the vestry for anybody and everybody to read. It is the poor man's commentary, the old Christian's companion, suitable for everybody, instructive to all. His own account of how he was led to write his exposition affords us an example of delighting in the law of the Lord:

> If any desire to know how so mean and obscure a person as I am, who in learning, judgement, felicity of expression, and all advantages for such a service am less than the least of all my Master's servants, came to venture upon so great a work, I can give no other account of it but this. It has long been my practice, what little time I had to spare in my study from my constant preparations for the pulpit, to spend it in drawing up expositions upon some parts of the New Testament, not so much for my own use as purely for my own entertainment, because I know not how to employ my thoughts and time more to my satisfaction. Every man that studies has some beloved study, which is his delight above any other; and this is mine. It is that learning which it was my happiness from a

child to be trained up in by my ever honoured father, whose memory must always be very dear and precious to me. He often minded me, that a good textuary is a good divine; and that I should read other books with this in my eye, that I might be the better able to understand and apply the Scripture.

You are aware, perhaps, that the latter part of the New Testament was completed by other hands, the good man having gone the way of all flesh. The writers were Messrs. Evans, Brown, Mayo, Bays, Roswell, Harriss, Atkinson, Smith, Tong, Wright, Merrell, Hill, Reynolds, and Billingsley – all Dissenting ministers. They have executed their work exceedingly well, have worked in much of the matter which Henry had collected, and have done their best to follow his methods, but their combined production is far inferior to Matthew Henry himself, and any reader will soon detect the difference.

Every minister ought to read Matthew Henry entirely and carefully through once at least. I should recommend you to get through it in the next twelve months after you leave college. Begin at the beginning, and resolve that you will traverse the goodly land from Dan to Beersheba. You will acquire a vast store of sermons if you read with your notebook close at hand; and as for thoughts, they will swarm around you like twittering swallows around an old gable towards the close of autumn. If you publicly expound the chapter you have just been reading, your people will wonder at the novelty of your remarks, and the depth of your thoughts, and then you may tell them what a treasure Henry is. Mr Jay's sermons bear indubitable evidence of his having studied Matthew Henry almost daily. Many of the quaint things in Jay's sermons are either directly traceable to Matthew Henry or to his familiarity with that writer. I have thought that the style of Jay was founded upon Matthew Henry: Matthew Henry is Jay writing, Jay is Matthew Henry preaching. What more could I say in commendation either of the preacher or the author?

John Calvin

It would not be possible for me too earnestly to press upon you the importance of reading the expositions of that prince among men, John Calvin. I am afraid that scant purses may debar you from their purchase, but if it be possible procure them, and meanwhile, since they are in the College library, use them diligently. I have often felt inclined to cry out with Father Simon, a Roman Catholic, 'Calvin possessed a sublime genius', and with Scaliger, 'Oh! How well has Calvin reached the meaning of the prophets – no one better'. You will find forty-two or more goodly volumes worth their weight in gold. Of all commentators I believe John Calvin to be the most candid. In his expositions he is not always what moderns would call Calvinistic; that is to say, where Scripture maintains the doctrine of predestination and grace he flinches in no degree, but inasmuch as some Scriptures bear the impress of human free action and responsibility he does not shun to expound their meaning in all fairness and integrity. He was no trimmer and pruner of texts. He gave their meaning as far as he knew it. His honest intention was to translate the Hebrew and the Greek originals as accurately as he possibly could, and then to give the meaning which would naturally be conveyed by such Greek and Hebrew words: he laboured, in fact, to declare, not his own mind upon the Spirit's words, but the mind of the Spirit as couched in those words. Dr King very truly says of him:

No writer ever dealt more fairly and honestly by the Word of God. He is scrupulously careful to let it speak for itself, and to guard against every tendency of his own mind to put upon it a questionable meaning for the sake of establishing some doctrine which he feels to be important, or some theory which he is anxious to uphold. This is one of his prime excellencies. He will not maintain any doctrine, however, orthodox and essential, by a text of Scripture which to him appears of doubtful application, or of inadequate force. For instance, firmly as he believed the doctrine of the Trinity, he refuses to

182

derive an argument in its favour from the plural form of the name of God in the first chapter of Genesis. It were easy to multiply examples of this kind, which, whether we agree in his conclusion or not, cannot fail to produce the conviction that he is at least an honest commentator, and will not make any passage of Scripture speak more or less than, according to his view, its divine Author intended it to speak.

The edition of John Calvin's works which was issued by the Calvin Translation Society is greatly enriched by the remarks of the editors, consisting not merely of notes on the Latin of Calvin, and the French translation, or on the text of the original Scriptures, but also of weighty opinions of eminent critics, illustrative manners and customs, and observations of travellers.

By the way, gentlemen, what a pity it is that people do not, as a rule, read the notes in the old Puritan books! If you purchase old copies of such writers as Brooks, you will find that the notes in the margins are almost as rich as the books themselves. They are dust of gold, of the same metal as the ingots in the centre of the page.

But to return to Calvin. If you need any confirmatory evidence as to the value of his writings, I might summon a cloud of witnesses, but it will suffice to quote one or two. Here is the opinion of one who is looked upon as his great enemy, namely, Arminius:

Next to the perusal of the Scriptures, which I earnestly incul-cate, I exhort my pupils to peruse Calvin's commentaries, which I extol in loftier terms than Helmich himself; for I affirm that he excels beyond comparison in the interpretation of Scripture, and that his commentaries ought to be more highly valued than all that is handed down to us by the Library of the Fathers; so that I acknowledge him to have possessed above most others, or rather above all other men, what may be called an eminent gift of prophecy.

Quaint Robert Robinson said of him: 'There is no abridging this sententious commentator, and the more I read him, the more does he become a favourite expositor with me.' Holy Baxter wrote, 'I know no man since the apostles' days whom I value and honour more than Calvin, and whose judgment in all things, one with another, I more esteem and come nearer to.'

Commenting

Having introduced you to the commentators, I must now press upon you one of the most practical uses of them, namely, your own public commenting upon the Scriptures read during divine service. Preaching in the olden time consisted very much more of exposition than it does now. I suppose that the sermons of the early Christians were for the most part expositions of lengthy passages of the Old Testament; and when copies of the Gospels, and the letters of Paul, had become accessible to the churches, the chief work of the preacher would be to press home the apostolic teachings by delivering an address, the backbone of which would be a complete passage of Scripture. There would probably be only faint traces of divisions, heads and points, such as we employ in modern discoursing, but the teacher would follow the run of the passage which was open before him, commenting as he read. I suppose this to have been the case, because some of the early Christian modes of worship were founded very much upon that of the synagogue. I say some of the modes, since I suppose that as the Lord Jesus left his disciples free from rubrics and liturgies, each church worshipped according to the working of the free Spirit among them; one with the open meeting of the Corinthians, and another with a presiding minister, and a third with a mixture of the two methods. In the synagogue, it was the rule of the Rabbis that never less than twenty-two verses of the law should be read at one time, and the preaching consisted of notes upon a passage of that length. Such a rule would be a mere superstition if we were slavishly bound by it, for the present plan of preaching from short texts, together with the great neglect of commenting publicly upon the Word, is very unsatisfactory. We cannot expect to deliver much of the teaching of Holy Scripture by picking verse by verse, and holding these up at random. The process resembles that of showing a house by exhibiting separate bricks. It would be an astounding absurdity if our friends used our private letters in this fashion, and interpreted them by short sentences disconnected and taken away from the context. Such expositors would make us out to say in every letter all we ever thought of, and a great many things besides far enough from our minds; while the real intention of our letters would probably escape attention. Nowadays, since expository preaching is not so common as it ought to be, there is the more necessity for our commenting during the time of our reading the Scriptures. Since topical preaching, hortatory preaching, experimental preaching, and so on – all exceedingly useful in their way – have almost pushed proper expository preaching out of place, there is the more need that we should, when we read passages of Holy Writ, habitually give running comments upon them.

Abstruse passages

I support my opinion with this reason, that the public reading of the abstruser parts of Scripture is of exceedingly little use to the majority of the people listening. I can recollect hearing in my younger days long passages out of Daniel, which might have been exceedingly instructive to me if I had obtained the remotest conception of what they meant. Take again, parts of the prophecy of Ezekiel, and ask yourselves what profit can arise from their perusal by the illiterate, 'unless some man shall guide them'. What more edification can come from a chapter in English which is not understood than from the same passage in Hebrew or Greek? The same argument which enforces translation demands exposition. If just a few explanatory words are thrown in by a judicious reader, it is wonderful how luminous obscure portions may be made. Two or three sentences will often reveal the drift of a whole chapter; the key of a great difficulty may be presented to the hearer in half-a-

185

score words, and thus the public reading may be made abundantly profitable. I once saw a school of blind children among the charming ruins of York Abbey, and could not help pitying their incapacity to enjoy so much beauty: how willingly would I have opened their eyes! Are ignorant people wandering among the glories of Scripture much less to be pitied? Who will refuse them the light?

Brief comments are helpful
Abundant evidence has come before me that brief comments upon Scripture in our ordinary services are most acceptable and instructive to our people. I have often heard from working men and their wives, and from merchants and their families, that my own expositions have been most helpful to them. They testify that when they read the Bible at home in the family, the exposition makes it doubly precious to them; and the chapter which they had unprofitably read in course at family prayers, when they peruse it the next time, recollecting what their minister has said upon it, becomes a real delight to them. The mass of our hearers, in London at least, do not, to any appreciable extent, read commentaries or any other books which throw a light upon the Scriptures. They have neither the money nor the time to do so, and if they are to be instructed in the Word of God in things which they cannot find out by mere experience, and are not likely to have explained to them by their associates, they must get that instruction from us, or nowhere else; nor do I see how we are to give them such spiritual assistance except through the regular practice of exposition.

Lesser points will find a place
Besides, if you are in the habit of commenting, it will give you an opportunity of saying many things which are not of sufficient importance to become the theme of a whole sermon, and therefore would probably remain unnoticed, to the great loss of the Lord's people and others. It is astonishing what a range of truth, doctrinal, practical, and experimental, Holy Scripture brings before us; and

equally worthy of admiration is the forcible manner in which that truth is advanced. Hints given in the way in which the Word of God offers them are always wise and opportune; as, for instance, the rebukes which the Word administers might have seemed too severe had they been made by the pastor, unsustained by the Word and unsuggested by it, but arising out of the chapter they cannot be resented. You can both censure sins and encourage virtues by dilation upon the stories which you read in the inspired records, whereas you might never have touched upon them had not the chapter read brought the matter before you. If you want to make full proof of your ministry, and to leave no single point of revelation untouched, your easiest mode will be to comment upon Scripture habitually. Without this, much of the Word will be utterly unknown to many of your people. It is a very sad fact that they do not read so much as they should at home; the ungodly, in England, scarcely read the Bible at all; and if only that part which we preach upon be expounded to them, how little of the Bible can they ever know! If you will mark your Bibles with lines under the texts from which you have spoken, as I have always done with an old copy which I keep in my study, you will discover that in twelve or fourteen years very little of the book has been gone through; a very large proportion of it remains unmarked, like a field unploughed. Try, then, by exposition to give your people a fair view of the entire compass of revelation; take them as it were to the top of Nebo, and show them the whole land from Dan to Beersheba, and prove to them that everywhere it flows with milk and honey.

The need for study

Earnestly do I advocate commenting. It is unfashionable in England, though somewhat more usual beyond the Tweed. The practice was hardly followed up anywhere in England a few years ago, and it is very uncommon still. It may be pressed upon you for one other reason, namely, that in order to execute it well, the commenting minister will at first have to study twice as much as the next preacher, because he will be called upon to prepare both his sermons and his expositions. As a rule, I spend much more time over the exposition than over the discourse. Once start a sermon with a great idea, and from that moment the discourse forms itself without much labour to the preacher, for a truth naturally consolidates and crystallizes itself around the main subject like sweet crystals around a string hung up in syrup; but as for the exposition, you must keep to the text, you must face the difficult points, and must search in to the mind of the Spirit rather than your own. You will soon reveal your ignorance as an expositor if you do not study; therefore diligent reading will be forced upon you. Anything which compels the preacher to search the grand old Book is of immense service to him.

The concordance
Fail not to be expert in the use of your concordance. Every day I live I thank God more and more for that poor half-crazy Alexander Cruden. Of course you have read his life, which is prefixed to the concordance; it exhibits him as a man of diseased mind, once or twice the inmate of a lunatic asylum, but yet for all that successfully devoting his energies to producing a work of absolutely priceless value, which never has been improved on, and probably never will be; a volume which must ever yield the greatest possible assistance to a Christian minister, being as necessary to him as a plane to the carpenter, or a plough to the husbands. Be sure you buy a genuine unabridged Cruden, and none of the modern substitutes. At the head of each notable word, Cruden gives you its meaning, and very often all its particular shades of meaning, so that he even helps you in sermonizing. When you have read his headings, by following out the concordance, you will observe connections in which the word occurs, which most advantageously and correctly fix its meaning. Thus will the Word of God be its own key.

Commentaries
Read commentaries! Yet be sure you use your own minds too, or the expounding will lack interest. Freshness, naturalness, life, will

188

always attract, whereas mere borrowed learning is flat and insipid. If you do not think and think much, you will become slaves and mere copyists. The exercise of your own mind is most healthful to you, and by perseverance, with divine help, you may expect to get at the meaning of every understandable passage. So to rely upon your own abilities as to be unwilling to learn from others is clearly folly; so to study others as not to judge for yourself is imbecility.

Explain difficult sentences
We must make sure in our public expositions that obscure and involved sentences are explained. To leap over difficulties, and only expound what is already clear, is to make commenting ridiculous. Your business is to make the Word plain. In Lombardy I observed great heaps of huge stones in the fields, which had been gathered out from the soil by diligent hands to make room for the crops; your duty is to 'gather out the stones', and leave the fruitful field of Scripture for your people to till. There are Orientalisms, metaphors, peculiar expressions, idioms, and other verbal memorabilia which arise from the Bible having been written in the East; all these you will do well to explain. To this end be diligent students of Oriental life. Let the geography of Palestine, its natural history, its fauna and flora, be as familiar to you as those of your own native village. Then as you read you will interpret the Word, and your flock will be fed thereby.

Apply the truth
The chief part of your commenting, however, should consist in applying the truth to the hearts of your hearers, for he who merely comprehends the meaning of the letter, without understanding how it bears upon the hearts and consciences of men, is like a man who causes the bellows of an organ to be blown, and then fails to place his fingers on the keys. It is of little service to supply men with information unless we urge upon them the practical inferences from them.

Never strain passages when you are expounding

Be thoroughly honest with the world: even if the Scriptures were the writings of mere men, conscience would demand fairness of you; but when it is the Lord's own Word, be careful not to pervert it even in the smallest degree. Let it be said of you, as I have heard a venerable hearer of Mr Simeon say of him, 'Sir, he was very Calvinistic when the text was so, and people thought him an Arminian when the text was that way, for he always stuck to its plain sense.'

A very sound neighbour of ours once said, by way of depreciating the grand old reformer, 'John Calvin was not half a Calvinist,' and the remark was correct as to his expositions, for in them, as we have seen, he always gives his Lord's mind and not his own.

In the church of St Zeno, in Verona, I saw ancient frescoes which had been plastered over, and then covered with other designs; I fear many do this with Scripture, daubing the text with their own glosses, and laying on their own conceits. There are enough of these plasterers about; let us leave the evil trade to them and follow an honest calling. Remember Cowper's lines –.

> A critic on the sacred text should be
> Candid and learn'd, dispassionate and free;
> Free from the wayward bias bigots feel,
> From fancy's influence and intemperate zeal;
> For of all arts sagacious dupes invent,
> To cheat themselves and gain the world's assent,
> The worst is – Scripture warped from its intent.

Use your judgement more than your fancy

Flowers are well enough, but hungry souls prefer bread. To allegorize with Origen may make men stare at you, but your work is to fill men's mouths with truth, not to open them with wonder.

Do not be carried away with new meanings

Plymouth Brethren delight to fish up some hitherto undiscovered tadpole of interpretation, and cry it round the town as a rare dainty;

let us be content with more ordinary and more wholesome fishery. No one text is to be exalted above the plain analogy of faith; and no solitary expression is to shape our theology for us. Other men and wiser men have expounded before us, and anything undiscovered by them it would be as well to put to the test and trial before we boast too loudly of the treasure trove.

Seek the Holy Spirit's aid

In all that I have said I have given you another reason for seeking the aid of the Holy Spirit. If you do not understand a book by a departed writer, you are unable to ask him his meaning, but the Spirit, who inspired Holy Scripture, lives for ever, and he delights to open up the Word to those who seek his instruction. He is always accessible: 'he dwelleth with you and shall be in you'. Go to him for yourselves and cry, 'Open thou mine eyes that I may behold wondrous things out of thy law'; and, this being granted you, entreat him to send his light and power with the Word when you expound it, that your hearers also may be led into all truth. Commentaries, expositions, interpretations, are all mere scaffolding; the Holy Spirit himself must edify you and help you to build up the church of the living God.

The great catastrophe

Church book entry for 19 October, 1856

On the evening of this day, in accordance with the resolution passed at the church meeting, 6 October, the church and congregation assembled to hear our Pastor in the Music Hall of the Royal Surrey Gardens. A very large number of persons (about 7,000) were assembled on that occasion, and the service was commenced in the usual way, by singing, reading the Scriptures, and prayer. Just, however, after our Pastor had commenced his prayer, a disturbance was caused (as it is supposed, by some evil-disposed persons acting in concert), and the whole congregation was seized with a sudden panic. This caused a fearful rush to the doors, particularly from the galleries. Several persons, either in consequence of their heedless haste, or from the extreme pressure of the crowd behind, were thrown down on the stone steps of the north-west staircase, and were trampled on by the crowd pressing upon them. The lamentable result was that seven persons lost their lives, and twenty-eight were removed to the hospitals seriously bruised and injured. Our Pastor, not being aware that any loss of life had occurred, continued in the pulpit, endeavouring by every means in his power to alleviate the fear of the people, and was successful to a very considerable extent. In attempting to renew the service, it was found that the people were too excited to listen to him, so the service was closed, and those who had remained dispersed quietly. This lamentable circumstance produced very serious effects on the nervous system of our Pastor. He was entirely prostrated for some days, and compelled to relinquish his preaching engagements.

Spurgeon's own account, published in 1857

Here the reader must pardon the writer if he introduces a personal narrative which is to him a most memorable proof of the lovingkindness of the Lord. Such an opportunity of recording my Lord's goodness may never again occur to me; and therefore now, while my soul is warm with gratitude for so recent a deliverance, let me lay aside the language of an author, and speak for myself, as I should tell the story to my friends in conversation. It may be egotism to weave one's own sorrows into the warp and woof of this meditation; but if the heart prompts the act, and the motions of the Holy Spirit are not contrary thereto, I think I may venture for this once to raise an Ebenezer in public, and rehearse the praise of Jesus at the setting thereof. Egotism is not such an evil thing as ungrateful silence; certainly, it is not more contemptible than mock humility. Right or wrong, here followeth my story.

On a night which time will never erase from my memory, large numbers of my congregation were scattered, many of them wounded and some killed, by the malicious act of wicked men. Strong amid danger, I battled against the storm; nor did my spirit yield to the overwhelming pressure while my courage could reassure the wavering, or confirm the bold; but when, like a whirlwind, the destruction was overpast, when the whole of its devastation was visible to my eye, who can conceive the anguish of my sad spirit? I refused to be comforted; tears were my meat by day, and dreams my terror by night.

I felt as I had never felt before. 'My thoughts were all a case of knives', cutting my heart in pieces, until a kind of stupor of grief ministered a mournful medicine to me. I could truly have said, 'I am not mad, but surely I have had enough to madden me, if I should indulge in meditation on it'. I sought and found a solitude which seemed congenial to me. I could tell my griefs to the flowers, and the dews could weep with me. Here my mind lay, like a wreck upon the sand, incapable of its usual motion. I was in a strange land, and a stranger in it. My Bible, once my daily food, was but a hand to lift the sluices of my woe. Prayer yielded not balm to me; in fact, my soul was like an infant's soul, and I could not rise to the dignity of supplication. 'Broken in pieces all asunder,' my thoughts, which had been to me a cup of delights, were like pieces of broken glass, the piercing and cutting miseries of my pilgrimage. I could adapt the words of Dr Watts, and say —

> The tumult of my thoughts
>   Doth but enlarge my woe;
> My spirit languishes, my heart
>   Is desolate and low.
> With every morning-light
>   My sorrow new begins:
> Look on my anguish and my pain,
>   And pardon all my sins.

Then came 'the slander of many' — barefaced fabrications, libellous insinuations, and barbarous accusations. These alone might have scooped out the last drop of consolation from my cup of happiness; but the worst had come to the worst, and the utmost malice of the enemy could do no more. Those who are already in the nethermost depths cannot sink lower. Misery itself is the guardian of the miserable. All things combined to keep me, for a while, in the darkness where neither sun nor moon appeared. I had hoped for a gradual return to peaceful consciousness, and I waited patiently for the dawning light. But it did not come as I had desired; for he who does for us exceeding abundantly above all that we ask or think sent me a happier answer to my requests. I had striven to think of the unmeasurable love of Jehovah, as displayed in the sacrifice of Calvary; I had endeavoured to muse upon the glorious character of the

194

exalted Jesus; but I found it impossible to collect my thoughts in the quiver of meditation, or, indeed, to place them anywhere but with their points in my wounded spirit, or else at my feet, trodden down in an almost childish thoughtlessness.

On a sudden, like a flash of lightning from the sky, my soul returned to me. The burning lava of my brain cooled in an instant. The throbbings of my brow were still; the cool wind of comfort fanned my cheek, which had been scorched in the furnace. I was free, the iron fetter was broken in pieces, my prison door was open, and I leaped for joy of heart. On wings of a dove, my spirit mounted to the stars – and beyond them. Whither did it wing its flight, and where did it sing its song of gratitude? It was at the feet of Jesus, whose name had charmed its fears, and placed an end to its mourning. The name – the precious name of Jesus – was like Ithuriel's spear, bringing back my soul to its own right and happy state. I was a man again, and what is more, a believer. The garden in which I stood became an Eden to me, and the spot was then most solemnly consecrated in my restored consciousness. Happy hour! Thrice-blessed Lord, who thus in an instant delivered me from the rock of my despair, and slew the vulture of my grief! Before I told to others the glad news of my recovery, my heart was melodious with song, and my tongue endeavoured tardily to express the music. Then did I give to my Well-beloved a song touching my Well-beloved; and oh, with what rapture did my soul flash out its praises! But all – all were to the honour of him, the First and the Last, the Brother born for adversity, the Deliverer of the captive, the Breaker of my fetters, the Restorer of my soul. Then did I cast my burden upon the Lord; I left my ashes, and arrayed myself in the garments of praise, while he anointed me with fresh oil. I could have riven the very firmament to get at him, to cast myself at his feet, and lie there bathed in the tears of joy and love. Never since the day of my conversion had I known so much of his infinite excellence, never had my spirit leaped with such unutterable delight. Scorn, tumult, and woe seemed less than nothing for his sake. I girded up my loins to run before his chariot, I began to shout out his glory, for my soul was absorbed in the one idea of his glorious exaltation and divine compassion.

After a declaration of the exceeding grace of God towards me, made to my dearest kindred and friends, I essayed again to preach. The task which I had dreaded to perform was another means of comfort, and I can truly declare that the words of that morning were as much the utterance of my inner man as if I had been standing before the bar of God. The text selected was in Philippians 2:9-11. May I trouble the reader with some of the utterances of the morning, for they were the unveilings of my own experience?

'When the mind is intensely set upon one object, however much it may, by diverse calamities, be tossed to and fro, it invariably returns to the place which it had chosen to be its dwelling place. You have noticed this in the case of David. When the battle had been won by his warriors, they returned flushed with victory. David's mind had doubtless suffered much perturbation in the meantime; he had dreaded alike the effects of victory and of defeat; but have you not noticed how his thoughts, in one moment, returned to the darling object of his affections? "Is the young man Absalom safe?" said he, as if it did not matter what else had occurred if only his favourite son were safe. So, beloved, it is with the Christian. In the midst of calamities, whether they be the wreck of nations, the crash of empires, the heaving of revolutions, or the scourge of war, the great question which he asks himself, and asks of others, too, is this – "Is Christ's Kingdom safe?" In his own personal afflictions, his chief anxiety is – Will God be glorified, and will his honour be increased by them? "If it is so," says he, "although I may be only like smoking flax, yet if the sun is not dimmed, I will rejoice; and though I may be a bruised reed, if the pillars of the temple are unbroken, what does it matter if I am bruised?" He finds it to be sufficient consolation, in the midst of all the breaking in pieces which he endures, to think that Christ's name stands fast and firm, and that, though the earth has reeled beneath his feet, yet Christ stands on a rock which can never be moved. Some of these feelings, I think, have crossed our minds. Amidst much tumult, and various rushings to and fro of troubling thoughts, our souls have returned to the dearest object of our desires, and we have found it no small consolation, after all, to say, "It does not matter what shall become of us; God has highly exalted *him*, and given *him* a name which is above every name; that at the name of *Jesus* every knee should bow." '

Thus is the thought of the love of Jesus, in his delivering grace, most indelibly impressed upon my memory; and the fact that this experience is to me the most memorable crisis of my life must be my apology for narrating it.

Selections from sermons

Accidents are not divine judgements

I have many times used the great calamity as an illustration of the truth that accidents are not to be regarded as divine judgements; perhaps the most notable instance is the sermon I preached soon after the collision in the Clayton tunnel on the Brighton railway. That discourse is to me the more memorable as I possess a copy of it which Dr Livingstone had carried with him in his African journeys, and on the top of which he had written *'Very good. – D.L.'* It was found, after his death, in the volume of his diary from November 1861 to July 1863, and was sent to me by his daughter, Mrs Livingstone-Bruce. In the course of the sermon I said:

'It has been most absurdly stated that those who travel on the first day of the week, and meet with an accident, ought to regard that accident as being a judgement from God upon them on account of their violating the Christian's day of worship. It has been stated, even by godly ministers, that the recent deplorable collision should be looked upon as an exceedingly wonderful and remarkable visitation of the wrath of God against those unhappy persons who happened to be in the Clayton tunnel. Now I enter my solemn protest against such an inference as that, not in my own name, but in the name of him who is the Christian's Master and the

Christian's Teacher. I say of those who were crushed in that tunnel, Suppose ye that they were sinners above all the other sinners? "I tell you, Nay: but, except ye repent, ye shall all likewise perish." Or those who were killed last Monday, think ye that they were sinners above all the sinners that were in London? "I tell you, Nay: but, except ye repent, ye shall all likewise perish." Now, mark, I would not deny that there have been judgements of God upon particular persons for sin; sometimes, and I think only exceedingly rarely, such things have occurred. Some of us have heard, in our experience, instances of men who have blasphemed God, and defied him to destroy them, who have suddenly fallen dead; and in such cases, the punishment has so quickly followed the blasphemy that one could not help perceiving the hand of God in it. The man had wantonly asked for the judgement of God, his prayer was heard, and the judgement came . . . But in cases of accident, such as that to which I refer, and in cases of sudden and instant death, again I say, I enter my earnest protest against the foolish and ridiculous idea that those who thus perish are sinners above all the sinners who survive unharmed. Let me just try to reason this matter out with Christian people; for there are some unenlightened Christians who will feel horrified by what I have said. Those who are ready at perversions may even dream that I would apologize for the desecration of the day of worship. Now, I do no such thing. I do not extenuate sin, I only testify and declare that accidents are not to be viewed as punishments for sin, for punishment belongs not to this world, but to the world to come. To all those who hastily look on every calamity as a judgement, I would speak in the earnest hope of setting them right.

'Let me begin, then, by saying, my dear brethren, do you not see that *what you say is not true*, and that is the best of reasons why you should not say it? Do not your own experience and observation teach you that one event happens both to the righteous and to the wicked? It is true, the wicked man sometimes falls dead in the street; but has not the minister fallen dead in the pulpit? It is true that a boat in which men were seeking their own pleasure on the

Sunday has suddenly gone down; but is it not equally true that a ship which contained none but godly men, who were bound upon an excursion to preach the Gospel, has gone down too? The visible providence of God has no respect of persons; and a storm may gather around the *John Williams* missionary ship, quite as well as around a vessel filled with riotous sinners. Why, do you not perceive that the providence of God has been, in fact, in its outward dealings, rather harder upon the good than upon the bad? For did not Paul say, as he looked upon the miseries of the righteous in his day, "If in this life only we have hope in Christ, we are of all men most miserable"? The path of righteousness has often conducted men to the rack, to the prison, to the gibbet, to the stake; while the road of sin has often led a man to empire, to dominion, and to high esteem among his fellows. It is not true that, in this world, God does, as a rule, and of necessity, punish men for sin, and reward them for their good deeds; for did not David say, "I have seen the wicked in great power, and spreading himself like a green bay tree"? And did not this perplex the psalmist for a little while, until he went into the sanctuary of God, and then he understood their end?'

'Will you allow me also to remark that the supposition against which I am earnestly contending is *a very cruel and unkind one*? For, if it were the case that all persons who thus meet with their death in an extraordinary and terrible manner were greater sinners than the rest, would it not be a crushing blow to bereaved survivors, and is it not ungenerous on our part to indulge the idea unless we are compelled by unanswerable reasons to accept it as an awful truth? Now, I defy you to whisper it in the widow's ear. Go home to her, and say, "Your husband was a worse sinner than the rest of men, therefore he died". You have not brutality enough for that. A little unconscious infant, which had never sinned, though, doubtless, an inheritor of Adam's fall, is found crushed amidst the debris of the accident. Now, think for a moment, what would be the infamous consequence of the supposition that those who perished were worse than others; you would have to make it out that this unconscious infant was a worse sinner than many in the dens of infamy whose lives are yet spared. Do you not perceive that the thing is radically false? And I might perhaps show you the injustice of it best by reminding you that it may, one day, turn upon your own head. Let it be your own case that you should meet with sudden death in such a way – are you willing to be adjudged to damnation on that account?

'Such an event may happen in the house of God. Let me recall to my own, and to your sorrowful recollection, what occurred when once we met together. I can say, with a pure heart, we met for no object but to serve out God, and the minister had no aim in going to that place but that of gathering many to hear who otherwise would not have listened to his voice; and yet there were funerals as a result of that holy effort (for holy effort still we avow it to have been, and the aftersmile of God has proved it so). There were deaths, and deaths among God's people – I was about to say, I am glad it was with God's people rather than with others. A fearful fright took hold upon the congregation, and they fled; and do you not see that, if accidents are to be viewed as judgements, then it is a fair inference that we were sinning in being there – an insinuation which our consciences repudiate with scorn? However, if that logic were true, it is as true against us as it is against others; and inasmuch as you would repel with indignation the accusation that any were wounded or hurt on account of sin in being there to worship God, what you repel for yourself repel for others, and be no party to the accusation which is brought against those who have been destroyed during the last fortnight, that they perished on account of any great sin.

'Here I anticipate the outcries of prudent and zealous persons who tremble for the ark of God, and would touch it with Uzzah's hand. "Well," says one, "but we ought not to talk like this, for it is a very serviceable superstition, because there are many people who will be kept from travelling on the Sunday by the accident, and we ought to tell them, therefore, that those who perished, perished because they travelled on Sunday." Brothers, I would not tell a lie to save a soul; and this would be telling lies, for it is not the fact. I would do anything that is right to stop Sunday labour and sin, but I would not forge a falsehood even to do that. They might have perished on a Monday as well as on a Sunday. God gives no special immunity any day of the week, and accidents may occur as well at one time as at another; and it is only a pious fraud when we seek thus to play upon the superstition of men to make capital for Christ. The Roman Catholic priest might consistently use such an argument; but an honest Christian man, who believes that the religion of Christ can take care of itself without his telling falsehoods, scorns to do it. These men did not perish because they travelled on a Sunday. Witness the fact that others perished on the Monday when they were on an errand of mercy. I know not why or wherefore God sent the accident. God forbid that we should offer our own reason when God has not given us his reason; but we are not allowed to make the superstition of men an instrument for advancing the glory of God. You know, among Protestants, there is a great deal of Popery. I meet with people who uphold infant baptism on the plea, "Well, it is not doing any hurt, and there is a great deal of good meaning in it, and it may do good; and even confirmation may be blessed to some people, therefore do not let us speak against it." I have nothing to do with whether the thing does hurt or not; all I have to do with is whether it is right, whether it is scriptural, whether it is true; and if the truth does mischief – which is a supposition we can by no means allow – that mischief will not lie at our door. We have nothing to do but to speak the truth, even though the heavens should fall.'

'I thank God that, terrible as the great catastrophe was, there was never in my experience another like it, for I do not think I could have survived a second one. I have, on several occasions, seen some cause for alarm when I have been conducting services in places that have not seemed to me to be able to stand the strain of the multitudes gathered to hear the Word; and the sensation I felt at the Surrey Gardens has, in a moment, come over me again. Many years ago, I was preaching in a building which was exceedingly crowded;

and, to my apprehension, there was a continuous tremor. I grew so anxious that I said to a friend, who understood such matters, "Go downstairs, and see whether this structure is really safe; for it seems hardly able to bear the weight of this crowd." When he returned, he looked anxious, but gave me no answer. The service ended quietly, and then he said, "I am so glad that everything has gone off safely. I do not think you should ever preach here again, for it is a very frail affair; but I thought that, if I frightened you, there would be more risk of a panic than there was in letting the service go on." The narrowest escape I ever had of a repetition of the Music Hall fatality was about eighteen months after the accident there; on the following Lord's Day morning – 11 April, 1858 – I thus described to my congregation the Lord's merciful interposition:

'During this week, my mind has been much directed to the subject of providence, and you will not wonder when I relate a portion of one day's story. I was engaged to preach, last Wednesday, at Halifax, where there was a heavy snowstorm. Preparations had been made for congregation of 8,000 persons, and a huge wooden structure had been erected. I considered that, owing to the severe weather, few persons could possibly assemble, and I looked forward to the dreary task of addressing an insignificant handful of people in a vast place. However, when I arrived, I found from 5,000 to 6,000 people gathered together to hear the word; and a more substantial-looking place it has not been my lot to see. It certainly was a great uncomely building; but, nevertheless, it seemed well adapted to answer the purpose. We met together in the afternoon, and again in the evening, and worshipped God; and we separated to our homes, or rather, we were about to separate, and all this while the kind providence of God was watching over us. Immediately in front of me there was a huge gallery, which looked an exceedingly massive structure, capable of holding 2,000 persons. This, in the afternoon, was crowded, and it seemed to stand as firm as a rock. Again, in the evening, there it stood, and neither moved nor shook. But mark the provident hand of God; in the evening, when the people were retiring, and when there were scarcely more than a hundred persons there, a great beam gave way, and down came a portion of the flooring of the gallery with a fearful crash. Several people were precipitated with the planks, but still the good hand of God watched over us, and only two persons were severely injured with broken legs, which it is trusted will be set so as to avoid the necessity of amputation. Now, had this happened any earlier, not only must many more have been injured, but there are a thousand chances to one, as we say, that a panic must necessarily have ensued similar to that which we still remember, and deplore as having occurred in this place. Had such a thing happened, and had I been the unhappy preacher on the occasion, I feel certain that I should never have been able to occupy the pulpit again. Such was the effect of the first calamity that I marvel that I ever survived. No human tongue can possibly tell what I experienced. The Lord, however, graciously preserved us; the fewness of the people in the gallery prevented any such catastrophe, and thus a most fearful accident was averted. But there is a more marvellous providence still to record. Overloaded by the immense weight of snow which fell upon it, and beaten by a heavy wind, the entire structure fell with an enormous crash three hours after we had left it, splitting the huge timbers into shivers, and rendering very much of the material utterly useless for any future building. Now mark this – had the snow begun three hours earlier, the hall must have fallen upon us, and how few of us would have escaped, we cannot guess. But mark another thing. All day long it thawed so fast that the snow as it fell seemed to leave a mass, not of white snow, but of snow and water together. This ran through the roof upon us, to our considerable annoyance, and I was almost ready to complain that we had hard dealings from God's providence. But if it had been a frost, instead of a thaw, you can easily perceive that the place must have fallen several hours before it did; and then your minister, and the greater part of his congregation, would probably have been in the other world. There may be some who deny providence altogether. I cannot conceive that there were any witnesses of that scene who could have done so. This I know, if I had been an unbeliever to this day in the doctrine of the supervision and wise care of God, I must have been a believer at this hour. Oh, magnify the Lord with me, and let us exalt his name together! He has been very gracious unto us, and remembered us for good.'

Farewell sermon

Mr Spurgeon preached on the occasion of the last service at the Surrey Gardens on the Lord's Day morning, December 11, 1859, from Paul's farewell to the Ephesian elders: 'Wherefore I take you to record this day, that I am pure from the blood of all men. For I have not shunned to declare unto you all the counsel of God.' That discourse so well summarizes his three years' ministry in the Music Hall that an extract from it may be appropriately inserted here:

'If any of us would clear our conscience by delivering all the counsel of God, we must take care that we preach, in the first place, *the doctrines of the Gospel*. We ought to declare that grand doctrine of Father's love towards his people from before all worlds. His sovereign choice of them, his covenant purposes concerning them, and his immutable promises to them, must all be uttered with trumpet tongue. Coupled with this, the true evangelist must never fail to set out the beauties of the person of Christ, the glory of his offices, the completeness of his work, and, above all, the efficacy of his blood. Whatever we omit, this must be in the most forcible manner proclaimed again and again. That is no Gospel which has not Christ in it; and the modern idea of preaching *the truth* instead of Christ is a wicked device of Satan. Nor is this all, for as there are three Persons in the Godhead, we must be careful that they all have due honour in our ministry. The Holy Spirit's work in regeneration, in sanctification, and in preservation, must be always magnified from our pulpit. Without his power, our ministry is a dead letter, and we cannot expect his arm to be made bare unless we honour him day by day.

205

'Upon all these matters we are agreed, and I therefore turn to points upon which there is more dispute, and consequently more need of honest avowal, because of more temptation to concealment. To proceed then: I question whether we have preached all the counsel of God unless predestination, with all its solemnity and sureness, be continually declared – unless election be boldly and nakedly taught as being one of the truths revealed by God. It is the minister's duty, beginning from the fountain-head, to trace all the other streams; dwelling on effectual calling, maintaining justification by faith, insisting upon the certain perseverance of the believer, and delighting to proclaim that gracious covenant in which all these things are contained, and which is sure to all the chosen, blood-bought seed.

'There is a tendency in this age to throw doctrinal truth in the shade. Too many preachers are offended with that siren truth which the Covenanters held, and to which the Puritans testified in the midst of a licentious age. We are told that the times have changed, that we are to modify these old (so-called) Calvinistic doctrines, and bring them down to the tone of the times; that, in fact, they need dilution, that men have become so intelligent that we must pare off the angles of our religion, and make the square into a circle by rounding off the most prominent edges. Any man who does this, so far as my judgement goes, does not declare all the counsel of God. The faithful minister must be plain, simple, pointed, with regard to these doctrines. There must be no dispute about whether he believes them or not. He must so preach them that his hearers will know whether he preaches a scheme of free will, or a covenant of grace – whether he teaches salvation by works, or salvation by the power and grace of God.

'But, beloved, a man might preach all these doctrines to the full, and yet not declare all the counsel of God. It is not enough to preach doctrine; we must preach *duty*, we must faithfully and firmly insist upon *practice*. So long as you will preach nothing but bare doctrine, there is a certain class of men, of perverted intellect, who will admire you; but once begin to preach responsibility – say

206

outright, once for all, that if the sinner perish, it is his own fault, that if any man sinks to hell, his damnation will lie at his own door, and at once there is a cry of "Inconsistency; how can these two things stand together?" Even good Christian men are found who cannot endure the whole truth, and who will oppose the servant of the Lord who will not be content with a fragment, but will honestly present the whole Gospel of Christ. This is one of the troubles that the faithful minister has to endure; but he is not faithful to God – I say it solemnly, I do not believe that any man is even faithful to his own conscience, who can preach simply the doctrine of sovereignty, and neglect to insist upon the doctrine of responsibility. I do assuredly believe that every man who sinks into hell will have himself alone to curse for it. The apostle Paul knew how to dare public opinion, and on one hand to preach the duty of man, and on the other the sovereignty of God. I would borrow the wings of an eagle, and fly to the utmost height of high doctrine when I am preaching divine sovereignty. God has absolute and unlimited power over men to do with them as he pleases, just as the potter does with the clay. Let not the creature question the Creator, for he has given no account of his matters. But when I preach concerning man, and look at the other aspect of truth, I dive to the utmost depth. I am, if you will so call me, a low doctrine man in that, for as an honest messenger of Christ I must use his own language, and cry, "He that believeth not is condemned already, because he hath not believed in the name of the only begotten Son of God".

'Moreover, if a man would declare all the counsel of God, and not shun to do so, he must be very outspoken concerning the crying sins of the times. The honest minister does not merely condemn sin in the mass, he singles out separate sins in his hearers; and without drawing the bow at a venture, he puts an arrow on the string, and the Holy Spirit sends it right home to the individual conscience. He who is true to his God looks to his congregation as separate individuals; and he endeavours to adapt his discourse to men's consciences, so that they will perceive he speaks of them. If there is a vice that you should shun, if there is an error that you should avoid, if there is a duty that you ought to fulfil, if all these things are not mentioned in the discourses from the pulpit, the minister has shunned to declare all the counsel of God. If there is one sin that is rife in the neighbourhood, and especially in the congregation, should the minister avoid that particular vice in order to avoid offending you, he has been untrue to his calling, dishonest to his God.

'But, then, let me remark further, the true minister of Christ feels impelled to preach the whole truth because it and it alone can meet the needs of man. The believer in Christ, if he is to be kept pure, simple, holy, charitable, Christ-like, is only to be kept so by the preaching of the whole truth as it is in Jesus. And as for the salvation of sinners, ah, my hearers, we can never expect God to bless our ministry to the conversion of sinners unless we preach the Gospel as a whole! Let me get but one part of the truth, and always dwell upon it to the exclusion of every other, and I cannot expect my Lord's blessing; but if I preach as he would have me preach, he will certainly own the word; he will never leave it without his own living witness. But let me imagine that I can improve the Gospel, that I can make it consistent, that I can dress it up and make it look finer, I shall find that my Master has departed, and the "Ichabod" is written on the walls of the sanctuary. How many there are kept in bondage through neglect of Gospel invitations! They go up to the house of God, longing to be saved, and there is nothing but predestination for them. On the other hand, what multitudes are kept in darkness through practical preaching! It is, "Do! Do! Do!" and nothing but "Do!" and the poor soul comes away and says, "What use is that command to me? I can do nothing. Oh, that I had the way of salvation pointed out as available for me!"

'I must now address to you a *very few earnest, sincere, and affectionate words by way of farewell*. I wish not to say anything in self-commendation; I will not be my own witness as to my faithfulness; but I appeal to you, I take you to witness this day, that "I have not shunned to declare unto you all the counsel of God". Often have I come into this pulpit in great weakness, and I have far more often

208

gone away in great sorrow, because I have not preached to you as earnestly as I desired. I confess to many errors and failings, and more especially to a lack of earnestness when engaged in prayer for your souls; but there is no charge of which my conscience acquits me, this morning, and I think you will acquit me, too, "for I have not shunned to declare unto you all the counsel of God". If in anything I have erred, it has been an error of judgement. I may have been mistaken; but, so far as I have learned the truth, I can say that no fear of public opinion, nor of private opinion, has even turned me aside from that which I hold to be the truth of my Lord and Master. I have preached to you the precious things of the Gospel. I have endeavoured, to the utmost of my ability, to preach grace in all its fullness; I know the preciousness of that doctrine in my own experience; God forbid that I should preach any other! If we are not saved by grace, we can never be saved at all. If, from first to last, the work of salvation be not in God's hands, none of us can ever see his face with acceptance. I preach this doctrine, not from choice, but from absolute necessity; for if this doctrine is not true, then we are lost souls; your faith is vain, our preaching is vain, and we are still in our sins, and there we must continue to the end. But, on the other hand, I can also say, I have not shunned to exhort, to invite, to entreat; I have bidden the sinners come to Christ. I have been urged not to do so, but I could not resist it. With bowels yearning over perishing souls, I could not conclude without crying, "Come to Jesus, sinner, come." With eyes weeping for sinners, I am compelled to bid them come to Jesus. It is not possible for me to dwell upon doctrine without invitation. If you do not came to Christ, it is not for want of calling, or because I have not wept over your sins, and travailed in birth for the souls of men. The one thing I have to ask of you is this – bear me witness, my hearers, bear me witness that, in this respect, I am pure from the blood of all men, for I have preached all that I know of the whole counsel of God. Have I known a single sin which I have not rebuked? Has there been a doctrine that I have believed which I have kept back? Has there been a part of the Word, doctrinal or experimental, which I have wilfully concealed? I am very far from perfect, again with weeping I confess my unworthiness, I not served God as I ought to have done, I have not been so earnest with you as I could have desired to be. Now that my three years' ministry here is over, I could wish that I might begin again, that I might fall on my knee before you, and beseech you to regard the things that make for your peace; but here, again, I do repeat it that, while as to earnestness I plead guilty, yet as to truth and honesty I can challenge the bar of God, I can challenge the elect angels, I can call you all to witness that I have not shunned to declare unto you all the counsel of God.

'In a little while, some of you may be frequenting places where the Gospel is not preached; you may embrace any other and a false gospel; I only ask this thing of you: Bear me witness that it was not my fault, that I have been faithful, and have not shunned to declare unto you all the counsel of God. Possibly, some here who have been restrained from evil by the fact of having attended a place of worship, seeing the chosen minister has gone, may not go anywhere else afterwards. You may become careless. Perhaps, next Sabbath day, you may be at home, lolling about, and wasting the day; but there is one thing I should like to say before you make up your mind not to attend the house of God again: Bear me witness that I have been faithful with you. It may be that some here, who have professedly run well for a time while they have been hearing the Word, may go back; some of you may go right into the world again, you may become drunkards, swearers, and the like. God forbid that it should be so! But I charge you, if you plunge into sin, do at least say this one thing for him who desired nothing so much as to see you saved: say I have been honest to you; that I have not shunned to declare unto you all the counsel of God. O my hearers, some of you in a little time will be on your dying beds! When your pulse is feeble, when the terrors of grim death are round about you, if you are still unconverted to Christ, there is one thing I shall want you to add to your last will and testament; it is this: the exclusion of the poor minister, who stands before you this day, from any share in that desperate folly of yours which has led you to neglect your own soul. Have I not implored you to repent? Have I not bidden you look to Christ before death surprises you? Have I not exhorted you, my hearers, to lay hold upon the hope set before you in the Gospel? O sinner, when you are wading through the black river, cast back no taunt on me as though I was your murderer, for in this thing I can say, "I wash my hands in innocence; I am clear of thy blood". But the day is coming when we shall all meet again; this great assembly will be merged into a greater one, as the drop loses itself in the ocean; and, in that day, if I have not warned you, if I have not preached Christ to you, and bidden you flee to him for refuge, then, though you perish, your soul will be required of me. I beseech you, if you laugh at me, if you reject my message, if you despise Christ, if you hate his Gospel, if you will be damned, yet at least give me an acquittal of your blood. I see some before me who do not often hear me; and yet I can say concerning them that they have been the subject of my private prayers; and often, too, of my tears, when I have seen them going on in their iniquities. Well, I do ask this one thing, and as honest men you cannot deny it me; if you will have your sins, if you will be lost, if you will not come to Christ, at least, amid the thunders of the last great day, acquit me of having helped to destroy your souls.

'What more can I say? How shall I plead with you? Had I an angel's tongue, and the heart of the Saviour, then would I plead; but I cannot say more than I have often done. In God's name, I beseech you, flee to Christ for refuge. If all has not sufficed before, let this suffice now. Come, guilty soul, and flee away to him whose wide-open arms are willing to receive every soul that flees to him in penitence and faith. In a little time, the preacher himself will lie stretched upon his bed. A few more days of solemn meeting, a few more sermons, a few more prayers, and I think I see myself in that upper chamber, with friends watching around me. He who has preached to thousands now needs consolation for himself; he who has cheered many in the article of death is now passing through the river himself. My hearers, will there be any of you, whom I shall see upon my death-bed, who will charge me with being unfaithful?

Will these eyes be haunted with the visions of men whom I have amused, and interested, but into whose hearts I have never sought to convey the truth? Shall I lie there, and shall these mighty congregations pass in dreary panorama before me; and as they subside before my eyes, one after the other, shall each one curse me as being unfaithful? God forbid! I trust will do me this favour, that, when I lie dying, you will allow that I am clear of the blood of all men, and have not shunned to declare unto you all counsel of God. Thunders such as have never been heard before must roll over this poor head, and lightnings more terrific than have ever scathed the fiend will blast this heart, if I have been unfaithful to you. My position – if I had but once preached the Word to these crowds, not to speak of many hundreds of times – my position would be the most awful in the whole universe if I were unfaithful. Oh, may God avert that worst of ills – unfaithfulness – from my head! Now, as I stand here, I make this my last appeal: "I pray you, in Christ's stead, be ye reconciled to God." But if ye will not be, I ask you this single favour – and I think you will not deny it me – take the blame of your own ruin, for I am pure from the blood of all men, since I have not shunned to declare unto you all the counsel of God.'

Books by C. H. Spurgeon

Spurgeon's regular sermons were published separately week by week by Passmore and Alabaster and were later collected into two series of bound volumes, *New Park Street Pulpit* and *Metropolitan Tabernacle Pulpit*. Large collections of his expository sermons were issued, some years after his death, under the titles *Treasury of the Old Testament* and *Treasury of the New Testament*. The following list includes other books written by Spurgeon, but excludes the many anthologies and other books which he edited:

All of grace: an earnest word with those who are seeking salvation ... 1886.
Around the wicket gate: or, A friendly talk with seekers concerning faith in the Lord Jesus Christ. 1884.
'Be of good cheer': the Saviour's comforting exhortation enlarged upon. 1881.
The Bible and the newspaper. 1878.
The cheque book of the Bank of Faith. 1888.
C.H. Spurgeon's autobiography, compiled from his diary, letters, and records by his wife and his private secretary. 4 vols. 1896–1900.
Christ's glorious achievements. 1877.
Christ's relation to his people. 1904.
'Come, ye children': a book for parents and teachers on the Christian training of children. 1897.
Commenting and commentaries: two lectures ... with a catalogue of biblical commentaries. 1876; reissued by the Banner of Truth Trust in 1969 with a complete textual index to Spurgeon's sermons.
Complete in Christ; and Love's logic. 1892.

A double knock at the door of the young. 1875.

Eccentric preachers. 1879.

Evening by evening: or, Readings at eventide for the family or the closet. 1868.

Everybody's book: the pilgrim's guide. 1898.

Faith: what it is and what it leads to. 1903.

Feathers for arrows: or, Illustrations for preachers and teachers. 1870.

Gleanings among the sheaves. 1864.

Glorious themes for saints and sinners. 1899.

A good start: a book for young men and women. 1898.

'Good tidings of great joy': Christ's incarnation the foundation of Christianity. 1901.

The Gospel of the Kingdom: a popular exposition of the Gospel according to Matthew. 1893.

Grace triumphant. 1904.

Infant salvation: a sympathetic word for bereaved parents. c.1870.

John Ploughman's pictures; or, More of his plain talk for plain people. 1880.

John Ploughman's talk; or, Plain advice for plain people. 1868.

Lectures to my students. 3 series. 1875–94.

Messages to the multitude: being ten representative sermons. 1892.

The Messiah: sermons on our Lord's names, titles and attributes. 1898.

The Metropolitan Tabernacle: its history and work. 1876.

Morning by morning: or, Daily readings for the family or the closet. 1870.

The mourner's comforter: being seven discourses upon Isaiah lxi. 1–3. 1878.

My sermon-notes: a collection from outlines of discourses. 4 vols. 1884–95.

The old Gospel and the new theology: twelve sermons. 1908.

'Only a Prayer-meeting!' Forty addresses at Metropolitan Tabernacle and other prayer-meetings. 1901.

Our Lord's passion and death: sermons. 1904.

The people's Christ, and other sermons. 1903.

Pictures from Pilgrim's Progress: a commentary on portions of John Bunyan's immortal allegory. 1903.

The pleasant catechism concerning Christ. 1865.

The present truth: a collection of sermons preached at the Metropolitan Tabernacle. 1883.

The saint and his Saviour: or, The progress of the soul in the knowledge of Jesus. 1857.

The salt-cellars: being a collection of proverbs together with homely notes thereon. 2 vols. 1889.

Sermons in candles. 1890.

Seven wonders of grace. 1877.

The soul-winner; or, How to lead sinners to the Saviour. 1895. *Storm signals being a collection of sermons.* 1885.

Teachings of nature in the kingdom of grace. 1896.

'Till he come': communion meditations and addresses. 1894.

Two letters from C.H. Spurgeon: one to the Evangelical Alliance, signifying his withdrawal from that association; and another to the Christian public, proving that his accusations . . . are neither novel nor singular. 1864.

What the stones say; or, Sermons in stones. 1894.

Words of advice for seekers. 1896.

Words of cheer for daily life. 1895.

Words of counsel for Christian workers. 1896.

Words of warning for daily life. 1895.

Words of wisdom for daily life. 1893.